There Must Be More Than This

Identity & Spiritual Renewal in the Kingdom of "Whatever"

A Letter to My Generation

DANIEL SCHWINDT

There Must Be More Than This

Identity and Spiritual Renewal in the Kingdom of "Whatever"

✦

A LETTER TO MY GENERATION

Angelico Press

First published in the USA
by Angelico Press 2015

For information, address:
Angelico Press, Ltd.
4709 Briar Knoll Dr. Kettering, OH 45429
www.angelicopress.com

Paperback: 978-1-62138-132-7
eBook: 978-1-62138-133-4

Cover design: Michael Schrauzer

CONTENTS

What I do unto the least of my brethren, that I do unto Christ. But what if I should discover that the least amongst them all, the poorest of all the beggars, the most impudent of all the offenders, the very enemy himself—that these are within me, and that I myself stand in need of the alms of my own kindness—that I myself am the enemy who must be loved—what then? As a rule, the Christian's attitude is then reversed; there is no longer any question of love or long-suffering; we say to the brother within us 'Raca,' and condemn and rage against ourselves. We hide it from the world; we refuse to admit ever having met this least among the lowly in ourselves. Had it been God himself who drew near to us in this despicable form, we should have denied him a thousand times before a single cock had crowed.

C. G. Jung

I often play against man, God says, but it is he who wants to lose, the idiot, and it is I who want him to win.
And I succeed sometimes
In making him win.

Charles Péguy

Foreword

Dear Reader,

This letter was written with a very specific audience in mind: one which shares, at least to some degree, my experience of life, my struggles, my doubts, and what you might call my spiritual idiosyncrasies.

This implies, almost automatically, that these pages will only really be accessible to those of my own generation and of my own country, which is the United States. Readers who fall outside those narrow limits will likely find very little truth or edification in what follows. They may find curiosities, confusions, and plenty of offenses, but they will not be able to comprehend or internalize the problems dealt with here. To those readers I can only apologize ahead of time, and say that, had I had them in mind at the start, I would have written a different book. Perhaps I will write such a book one day, addressed to members of some generation or nation far removed from my own.

Here and now, however, I speak mainly to my own cohort. It is their situation which concerns me most, because it is my situation, and because I believe that my generation has a very unique fate, and thus a very unique opportunity. I believe that we so-called "Millennials" were born at a rare culmination of social, political, and spiritual tension—a brief period of chaos when old things fall apart and new things are born.

This means that, like it or not, the collective energies my generation brings to bear on this world will have consequences much more profound and far-reaching than would normally be possible during periods of stability and peace. Thus, our situation is a precarious one because it asks us to endure the sense of chaos and unrest that accompanies all times of transition, while simultaneously placing at our feet the responsibility of giving birth to something new.

The difficulties felt by men and women under these conditions are necessarily unique, and so this letter is my attempt to bring comfort to my comrades, hopefully easing some small amount of our shared confusion, by describing what I myself have seen and explaining where I plan to go.

And one final note concerning what follows: the word *elders* will be used throughout this letter, usually with a negative connotation and without qualification. Although I will use it in such a way, it is not meant as a generalization. I know many men and women, much older and wiser than I, who work to guide the lives of young people with utmost concern and loving counsel. However, there are also a substantial number of individuals who would attribute all the woes of the current era to young people exclusively, abandoning entirely their post as wise guides for an inexperienced youth. Their mantra is a scornful "Kids these days!" It is to this group that the term *elders* is meant to apply in this particular letter. I use the term in this way, as if speaking generally and universally, simply because it would be monotonous to explain each time that I mean only our disdainful critics. The reader must not forget this, because to dishonor in general those older than oneself is a great injustice, not only to one's elders, but even to one's own well-being. The commandment about honoring thy father and mother was a piece of twofold wisdom, necessary for the sanity of both child and parent. Nothing will fill you with more bitterness and turmoil than to harbor hatred for those who gave birth to you. Thus, you may only break the commandment to your own wounding. Neither do I intend to break it here.

DANIEL SCHWINDT

Our Agnosticism

> It seems to us that God has died of old age, and we exist without a goal. . . . We are not embittered; we start from zero. We were born among the ruins. When we were born, the gold was already transmuted into lead.
>
> Paul van den Bosch[1]

THE ESSENTIAL CHARACTERISTIC of our generation is a deep-seated, almost fundamental, *agnosticism*. I do not mean the type of agnosticism that is acknowledged and professed as a conscious decision someone has reached about the world or about a god. I'm not referring to anyone's "convictions." Our agnosticism is not so much about religion as about things in general, although religion is of course included. We entertain a basic uncertainty about people, traditions, and institutions, and especially about ourselves.

It is not a "willful" agnosticism. We would believe if we could —maybe not in God, but at least in *something*—because belief represents certainty, and certainty represents comfort. We long for that comfortable rootedness and security. We just can't seem to find it; and if we do find it, we can't seem to maintain it for any period of time.

It is as if all those notions that our forefathers took as "common sense" and "self-evident" are now almost impossible for us to grasp. We can touch them momentarily but not hold them. We grab at them and they evaporate from our closed fists. What-

1. Paul van den Bosch, *Les Enfants de l'absurde: Essai* (Paris: La Table Ronde, 1956), 13, 17.

ever faculty it is that allows "faith" to take root in a man, insulating him from doubt about his existence, has atrophied in us. Many of us try for years to hold on to the traditions of our parents and our society, but sooner or later find the effort too taxing. We become exhausted and collapse, and then we lie inert from the exertion.

Therefore, it must be understood that I use the term *agnostic* in its broadest sense, with very little spiritual or moral connotation. I use it to describe an elementary human condition. I apply it universally to our generation, because I perceive it universally.

Whether the individual happens to be Christian, atheist, or even a consciously professed "agnostic," it matters little to me. He is a member of the agnostic generation. That is us, dear reader—you and I.

I want to clarify further that I use the term without imputing any guilt. It isn't the kind of agnosticism that comes after a person "rejects God." We are agnostics fundamentally, not necessarily by any particular conviction. It is actually quite the opposite of a conviction: we are agnostics by our utter incapacity to maintain any sort of conviction about anything. The claim that something might be true "once and for all" presents serious, often insurmountable, difficulties for us, and we reject it almost instinctively.

We cannot take anything on faith. We cannot give anyone the benefit of the doubt, because we cannot even give it to ourselves.

Some lament "moral relativism," thinking that this is the spiritual plague which characterizes our condition. They bombard us with arguments about "right" and "wrong," trying to convince us that these things do exist and that they are certainties. But again, we don't have certainties—that is what they miss, and that is why they miss the whole point. They think that the relativism of our generation is a *cause* of something, but it is an *effect*, and a very late effect at that. It is the inevitable result of our state. It is the only moral philosophy we could possibly maintain—it is the philosophy of "I don't know."

One more thing: what I've said so far applies more to knowledge than to passions. When I say that we cannot maintain convictions, I do not mean that we are heartless—quite the opposite! We have passions, sometimes white-hot passions, but they are never centered on anything absolute.

Our generation, we fight for "causes," and not beliefs. They are often very worthy causes, but they are still not convictions. We always stop short.

We'll fight for our neighbors too. Again, we *do* have hearts and a great depth of feeling. We are great humanitarians, and that is perhaps one of our most respectable qualities. But we won't fight for any particular truth about our neighbor. We just fight for him when we feel he is suffering injustice. Sometimes we get confused, however, because justice requires absolutes. We don't have absolutes, so we don't always know what we are fighting for. Nonetheless, we are willing to fight. That's my point—that we're fighters.

✦

So that's where we are, you and I and our contemporaries. I won't try to explain how things reached this point. That would require too much space, too much time, and it isn't my concern in this letter. I only want to state things as I see them and try to get our bearings. I needed to start with this fundamental characteristic, this *existential agnosticism*, because it is our generational starting point. We are born in doubt.

Doubt is a miserable starting point, I admit, because doubt is paralyzing. It can render you inert, and it takes a massive effort of the will to overcome this paralysis which is our constant mental companion. It's a miracle we get out of bed in the morning. So this is where we must begin—we must begin from zero.

Our Shame

> . . . whichever way you look at it, I was always guilty in the first place, and what is most vexing is that I was guilty without guilt, by virtue of the laws of nature.
>
> Fyodor Dostoyevsky[2]

OUR AGNOSTICISM can be easily seen because it is a difficulty of the mind; but we also have a second trait which is imbedded in another region, more subtle than thought, which we call the *conscience*. It is not so much known as felt, and I will, for lack of a better word, call it *shame*.

It is that desperately masked but undeniable tinge of guilt which, like our agnosticism, seems to color everything our gen-

2. Fyodor Dostoyevsky, *Notes from Underground* (New York: Penguin, 2004), 89.

eration does or creates. I see it in our music and in our art; I see it in our revolutions; it underpins even our most trifling pursuits. And what makes it so peculiar is that we were apparently born that way, somehow at fault just for existing, as if the doctor slapped us in the delivery room, not so that we would take a first breath, but rather to teach us a lesson for having misbehaved, and for coming out of our little rooms before we were told.

Those, therefore, who condemn our generation as "shameless" do not know how right they are, and in what way! If our shame is, as Dostoevsky said, a *guiltless guilt*, there from the start, then shamelessness is the only possible reaction.

To say it another way, having come to feel our guilt as a start rather than a finish, as the beginning rather than as the end result of some crime, our sense of justice is immediately thrown askew.

So where does this come from? Where is its seat within us? Is there really no cause? We must find one—or else we risk insanity.

Please, my earnest reader who happens to be Christian, do not spiral off now into speeches about original sin and fallen man. We get quite enough of that, most of us. Do not misunderstand me: we'll talk about original sin and other such things, but we'll do it later. Right now I just need you to sit quietly and wait your turn.

So anyway, that's what this letter is about, in addition to our disbelief. It's about us and our shame. These things can be explained only by explaining you to *yourself*, and me to *myself*.

That's the oldest path to wisdom, is it not? "Know thyself!" That's what the oracle told Socrates. That's the beginning. So let's begin there, at the beginning, with what we may know about ourselves.

And the first thing we can know about ourselves is that we were born guilty, not of original sin, or at least not of that only, but of something *worse*. We're guilty of shattering dreams. Having been born at this particular place and time, we are predestined to give the lie to a thousand false hopes—false hopes upon which an entire civilization was built. Like reluctant and unwilling Messiahs, we've come at the "fullness of time" to bring about something new, and we cannot help but be crucified for such a crime. I don't draw the analogy to make us sound noble. We are *unwilling* and usually *unwitting*, but we were born at this time and so that's that.

What has been for many generations a great stock of dreams will collapse under your feet. You won't know what's happening or why—but it will all be your fault. It all *is* your fault, because you were born here, and now. That's our tragedy and the wellspring of our shame. It's also the wellspring of our agnosticism, by the way. The two are Siamese twins woven into our generational soul. Our project is to extricate them from the spiritual tapestry, because they are poisoning the whole project, making it ugly; and unless we deal with the problem we'll never get anywhere.

The Silver Spoon

If you are to believe what you've been told by your elders, then one thing is certain: you were born with a "silver spoon in your mouth." You have things better than anyone ever has before—you are at the height of civilization, born in the greatest nation in the world (that's America, by the way). That's your great privilege. So why, then, do you feel cursed?

For starters, who wants a silver spoon in their mouth? You can't eat a spoon, and silver is indigestible. What do I care about a silver spoon unless it has something substantial and nourishing on the end of it? Does yours have something on the end of it, dear reader? Mine didn't. It was just there: cold, shiny, and hard. That's us, you and I, with our silver spoons.

We'd have settled for wooden spoons though, eh? All we really ever wanted was the soup that was supposed to be in the thing. But instead we were born and had these shiny silver things shoved into our mouths. When we quietly asked about the missing soup, we learned that such questions were profoundly ungrateful. "We gave you silver and you ask for soup! You're a spoiled lot, aren't you!" All the while, these things are being waved in our faces as we are told how grateful we should be for the nasty metallic aftertaste.

You needn't be grateful, dear reader—not for this. You do have things to be thankful for, things that have been handed down to you by your elders. We must never deny that. But what is worthy of your gratitude and what isn't are not great mysteries. You can see them for yourself, and judge them accordingly. You don't need anyone else telling you where to heap your gratitude. Save your thanks for a worthy cause. Our ancestors left us plenty of things to be thankful for; but this silver spoon, I'm sorry to say, is not one of them. And even if it is, we've got to admit that there is a strange overemphasis of the worth of this cold, shiny thing.

When were you last belittled because you did not have a proper appreciation for Homer's *Odyssey*? When was the last time you were scolded for not having taken advantage of the insights offered by the histories of Rome or Egypt? Why don't our elders shame us for these crimes? Why is it that the only time we are perceived as ungrateful children, it is because we do not love our electronics more?

Oh, how I'd love to be lectured on having neglected our rich heritage of poetry and art. That is a guilt I could embrace and act upon! That is a shame I could accept with contrition, because it is true of our generation.

We could accept that reproach and then we could go from there, making ourselves better and wiser men for our scolding! But we hear nothing of the sort. The shame laid at our feet is of an entirely different nature, so different that my little lament here is almost humorous in comparison.

This is my wish for you: that next time you are accused of being "ungrateful" for your silver spoon, that you would acknowledge your ingratitude wholeheartedly, and in doing so disarm ever so slightly your shame. You would pull its teeth by admitting the fact, if you were truly able to do so.

Don't deny it when it comes. Say to the spoon-giver: "Yes, I am ungrateful. Get that thing away from me." And then go about your business. If I can unburden you of at least that much guilt—one teaspoon full—then we've taken a step in the right direction, have we not?

✦

Is my spoon analogy growing old? Fine. As you know perfectly well, I'm talking about *wealth*. You were born in one of the wealthiest nations in the world, but you knew that already, because all your life you've seen people dancing in the streets, playing tambourines, chanting the fact.

That spoon is your iPhone and your HDTV and the car that was given to you at sixteen or whenever. It is your sedation dentistry, your Red Bull, your McDouble, and all the various things flaunted in front of you while you are reminded how lucky you are.

These are the things you *must* appreciate, if you want to pass through the tambourine frenzy without being turned against and torn apart. But you can't. Try as we may, we can't appreciate them as deeply and as fully as we are told that we should, and the reason is simple: these things aren't appreciable! You can't deeply appreciate a radio or a cell phone. It isn't human. You can become addicted to those things. You can become obsessed with a television, and dependent on fast food, but you can't appreciate them as if they were a symphony or a cathedral or a Monet.

If you could, then I wouldn't be writing you this letter. You'd be lost to me. When humanity is some day able to appreciate the luxury of a laptop with the depth that men once appreciated Bach, then mankind is extinct.

So I praise your ingratitude and your inability to appreciate these things, even if others condemn you for it. That is my hope that humanity still lives in you. Even if I must watch a dozen of our generation sit at a table in silence, each glued to his "mobile device," I know that, addicted as we are to these things, we do not *appreciate* them. Thank God for that.

Enough with the silver spoon then. Wealth is really just the beginning—just a superficiality. It was just a jumping-off point in my attempt to strip the first layer from that big "guilt onion" you're carrying around. We've still got to work on our havoc-ridden sense of justice that seems to be firing off at all the wrong times, always pointed directly back at us. I've got to get you to stop shooting yourself in the conscience, dear reader. A man should only have shame after having done something, so why is ours omnipresent? Why is it felt as a *pre-existent fact*, and not a *result*? We must go deeper than material possession.

The American Dream

THE ENTIRE FRAMEWORK into which you were born was constructed around a very specific set of assumptions. The idea was that if "the plan" was followed without deviation—if the ideology was obeyed with proper zeal—then a paradise would follow as a divine guarantee.

We might say that you were born into a new Israel, with a new covenant, a new Law, and, most importantly, a new promise. The new covenant is called the "American Way," while its promise is called the "American Dream," and these two combined will lead one to a life of peace and joy in the land of milk and honey.

The formula really was foolproof: work at least 40 hours a week for 40 years (or was it 80?), buy a house with a mortgage, own a couple of cars, go to church, pick a political party, vote for your guy and hate the other guy, be patriotic, fight in the wars that may come up, buy stuff—do all of these things and the Heavenly City will arise around you. This is faith and the great hope of our parents, and it is the inheritance of our generation.

But then there came something of a great catastrophe. The milk and honey began to dry up: foreclosures, perpetual war, divorce, unemployment, appalling political candidates, education that just makes children dumber, and on top of all that an undeniable feeling of aimlessness spreading through the entire nation. The people became surprised, and then confused, and then terrified. (Few thought to question the possibility that the milk and honey were never really there in the first place, despite the reality that many had never seen any.) They began to look around for what—or who—was to blame. Like the sailors on Jonah's ship, they knew that only a great sin could have called down such a wrathful storm.

In a crisis, men will have their heretics. Well, dear reader, that's you and I. We're the heretics of the New Covenant. Isn't that something? Now we are not only unwilling Messiahs, but also unwilling heretics! But I suppose the Messiah himself was a heretic, so our story may turn out alright after all. We're the Jonahs on this ship called "Liberty, Justice, Etc." The fact that we were born right on the ship's deck, long after the storm was already blowing, matters little to the confused crew.

But that's what happened. We came walking into the Promised Land just in time to see the milk go sour and the honey turn to dust. We were as shocked as anyone else. Why wouldn't we be? We were following the program—we hadn't doubted the faith, most of us. We had no ill intent. We even went to college and got our degrees! We've got bills to pay too, and big ones. But the catastrophe came, and the nation grew confused. We turned to our elders with questioning eyes, looking for guidance, and it was then that we realized our circumstances. The promise was failing and a traitor had to be found.

That is the heart of it, dear reader—that is our great shame. We're marked as destroyers of a faith because we were born when that faith was imploding on itself. If it were just our "lack of appreciation" for our material trinkets, we'd get over it, like any spoiled child. But when youths are accused of doing violence to the faith of their fathers—of preventing the earthly Paradise from coming—well, that's something a bit deeper, isn't it?

We were born at the collapse of a great edifice, and the weight of that collapse hangs over our heads every day. We hear about it in the news and on the streets. "Young people these days!" I heard it a thousand times before I was ever of an age to be considered a "young person."

Our predecessors believed so fervently in an illusion, in that great edifice and its promise; and we are, thanks to bad timing, dashing their hopes on the rocks by our very existence. Our fathers and our fathers' fathers clung to those chimeras so fiercely, and false hopes held that tight cannot be anything but blinding. The hope became the very identity of the nation. To question the hope was to question themselves—to deny the hope, well-nigh inconceivable. They simply could not accept any possibility that the promise was empty.

When the lookouts began crying "rocks ahead" they blamed the ocean, and now that the hull is tearing and the water rushing in, they are blaming the young crew. The course was perfect!—that was their great conviction—and so the blame *must* lie with the crew. That's you and I; we are the incompetent crew of this great barge with no reverse and no ability to turn left or right. Why would a perfect ship with a perfect course need to turn? Turning is heresy, you lazy villain! So we scramble, we go to school, we try to find jobs; but we know we are headed for the rocks with nothing to do but take the blame as the ship falls apart.

We are the disappointment of our fathers. That was our inevitable destiny—a destiny of disappointment. It has come to us to do what young people are never supposed to have to do: to prove that the wisdom of our predecessors was wrong. And even in this we are unwilling. Through all this we've made it clear we didn't want rebellion. Rebellion belongs to the ages before us, from 1776 up to the 60's.

We aren't rebels—we are simply dealing with the consequences of rebellion. That is the source of our dismay. We aren't trying to prove anyone wrong. Most of us are working our hands to the bone to keep the ship afloat. But it is sinking anyway, *and we are ashamed*. We are the crew that sunk the Titanic, and live with that responsibility. It is like a scar on us, except that it isn't something we gained through action—it is more of a birth mark. We've always had it.

And things will only get worse. As the ships sinks further, more and more will be placed at your feet by your elders, and by everyone. Even as the water rises to their necks they'll be accusing you of mutiny. That's the insanity of misplaced convictions, of zealous faith in a lie—it becomes hermetically sealed. Even if it starts off healthy and alive, it allows for no flow of air or life in or out. It just sits there. Your elders think you are destroying their hermetically-sealed faith, and you have to live with that. You only have one option, really. Leave them to their insanity.

Do you understand now why you might feel a tinge of existential shame, and why this can and must be discarded? You are giving the lie to the delusions of an ideological empire. You are a fantastic disappointment. But, while he who plays the role of revealing a lie may draw hatred on himself, there is a second implication: he who reveals a lie can only do so by bringing out the truth. He *is* disappointment for the false hopes, but he *is* himself a new hope which can take the place of the dead one. Along with your destiny of shame, you have a small spark of light that you brought with you into this world.

Tradition

> Tradition means giving votes to the most obscure of all classes, our ancestors. It is the democracy of the dead. Tradition refuses to submit to that arrogant oligarchy who merely happen to be walking around.
>
> G.K. Chesterton[3]

> I set out on this ground which I suppose to be self-evident, "that the earth belongs in usufruct to the living"; that the dead have neither powers nor rights over it.
>
> Thomas Jefferson[4]

WHAT MAKES AMERICA unique is that it is almost wholly the product of revolution. Many other nations have revolted here

3. G.K. Chesterton, *Orthodoxy* (Peabody: Hendrickson, 2006), 43.

4. Thomas Jefferson to James Madison, September 6, 1789, *Thomas Jefferson: Writings* (New York: Penguin, 1984), 959.

and there, to be sure, such as Scotland against England in the legendary days of William Wallace, but they were not fighting so that they could be born—they were fighting to return to a life they had had previously. They were revolting that they might return to their tradition and live it without interference.

For America this is not the case, since it was fighting not for a return but for a beginning. After the dust settled, the only tradition in the land was that of the native peoples, and this the revolutionaries had no intention of preserving. They had their own ideas, which they implemented, and which were of an entirely experimental character. They were not new ideas, to be sure; but they were novel in the sense that, while previous civilizations were aware of these ideas, they did not find them worthy of application.

Please understand that I have not pronounced judgment on any particular principle; our only purpose here is to observe one thing: that America is fundamentally anti-traditional, and therefore cannot be said to have any "traditions" of its own in any real sense. This is important to our subject because tradition, regardless of what you think of its merits, is a stabilizing force. It grounds people and gives them direction and identity. It does this even if it is a completely barbaric tradition. And so that is my point: we are a generation without traditions, and it trips us up at every moment.

We must also deal with a great irony here, because we've had a lot of ideas, words, and practices waved in front of us all our lives; and these things, we have been told, are the "American Tradition." Is that not the most profound hypocrisy? Have we already forgotten that the founding principles of our nation amounted to the rejection of all political tradition, and that much of the early progress of our American civilization amounted to the obliteration of the ancient traditions of a native people? How can we then wield the term "tradition" as if it were something which demanded respect and adherence? How can we speak of "tradition" as if it were inviolable and divine, when our civilization was born through its violation?

Our nation was born by rejecting the traditions of Europe while at the same time trampling over the traditions of a native civilization, and so America was born devoid of tradition and has quite possibly doomed itself to remain as such. America, we might say, is *anti*-traditional.

So, then, what about these ideas that were taught to us as our "tradition?" How are we to deal with them? What are they?

They were *conventions*, which are entirely different things: they are temporary, mediocre, subjective, shallow. They were political preferences, party allegiances, hollow economic ideologies, vague moral sentiments, disgraceful material aspirations. That's how we knew they weren't really traditions. Nothing we could sink our teeth into. They were already stale by the time they were told to us. Traditions don't grow stale. William Wallace fought to return to a tradition. Which one of us would fight to return to the New Deal, or for Reaganomics? The thought is laughable.

Tradition isn't something that old people hold in front of young people to show them how wrong they are. Well, it can be that, but that is not all that it is; and if that is the only way it survives then it isn't worthy of survival. A tradition is a gift, a truth, a light, and a support, and when it is real it can be seen by everyone in the community as such. That's how it becomes tradition: *because it is nothing more than wisdom in its simplest expression.*

But we don't have any of those things, those ancient and proven expressions of wisdom. Our predecessors wiped tradition off the map centuries ago and have been reeling ever since.

Of course, they couldn't reel for long. They couldn't live without traditions, even though they rejected every last one. And so they are constantly trying to construct a new framework from the rubble of their dynamite job. That was the technique of the Founders, after all. They took a sermon here, a platitude there, some Aristotle, some Cicero, far too much of Descartes, and even some St. Paul. With these they built the haphazard and wobbly thing we now see before us, which they now call the "American Tradition."

It is a grotesque piece of cultural-spiritual infrastructure, and the worst is that it keeps changing because its foundations will always lie in revolution. Always revolution, and so the structure quakes, ready to collapse at any moment and kill anyone who is standing inside.

Men are able to believe in this structure, this great counterfeit-tradition, for a very simple, psychological reason: because it is theirs. Its existence flatters, and its success affirms, and so their self-worth rests in its continued existence and its success. That is the most lethal and deceiving aspect of our traditions. They are changeable and so they change with each generation, sometimes becoming entirely reborn, sometimes becoming entirely perverted. Each builds its own revision of the tradition, which is always in its own image. It is a reflection of the deepest hopes and desires of whoever created it, and in that it is extremely dangerous.

That is why we must see them as *conventions*, and as something to always question and be wary of, and decidedly not as *tradition*, which is something so time-proven as to seem "pre-historic," in the precise sense of the term. Traditions aren't made—they just *are*, and you either take them or you don't, and you suffer or benefit accordingly. You either keep them or lose them, in which case you have to return to them in order to regain them. *But you never build them.*

Tradition is the result of men attempting to live to the full through ages, building bridges of beauty, wisdom, and soul, which then serve as paths to safely guide their young across the abyss. Conventions are blind inroads out over the precipice—like those old cartoon characters who would walk off a cliff and not fall until they looked down and realized where they were standing. You might get lucky with a convention, but it is always an experiment.

That is why it is a great deceit to sell conventions as traditions. It isn't the same product. One is proven, the other is just a first prototype that might explode in your face. This, dear reader, is how you must come to understand American "tradition." It is not a bridge, because it was made by burning bridges. Because of this you should not accept such conventions without question, as if they were immortal principles. You can take them or leave them.

Yes, you may take them if you want, these conventions. My purpose here is not to dissuade you from using them if you find them helpful, noble, or true. My purpose is not to disparage your whole American heritage. My purpose is only to call things what they are and call for an end to the exaggerations and the deifications. Feel free to hold to the philosophy of the Founders, but you must stop holding it as a *dogma*. Do you like the Constitution? Then defend it, even in the name of God, if you wish, but don't let anyone tell you that God wrote it with his own hand.

That's where the dangers and the perversions come in. Once you make these frail things into something divine, then you give them power over your soul and your conscience. And since our "traditions" are often just the preferences of those immediately before us, then you've given your soul over to a collection of petty aspirations, secular mythologies, and prejudices of a single generation. That's a dangerous game, to say the least. You allow politics and methodology to play at divinity, and you give them access to an area of yourself in which they have no business meddling. You give them the keys to your own soul and your own conscience.

Then one day you'll find yourself listening to your party leader as if he were Moses, and you'll be hating the other guy as if he were the anti-Christ. You'll be doing this because "the tradition" is under attack. All the while you'll live in agony and shame, because you sold your soul to *convention*.

This is the second layer of shame I want to peel off of your conscience. This is the second layer gone hard, dry, and calloused. When you are accused of despising convention, of having "no respect for tradition," you can save your guilt. You have not committed this crime. You aren't rejecting tradition; you are just rejecting the opinions of the person standing in front of you. That's what American tradition is: it is novelty and opinion, which is to say, it is *anti-tradition*.

Learn to see these counterfeit traditions for what they are, and discard this layer of your shame for good.

Freedom

> Free, dost thou call thyself? Thy ruling thought would I hear of, and not that thou hast escaped from a yoke. Art thou one entitled to escape from a yoke? Many a one hath cast away his final worth when he hath cast away his servitude. Free from what? What doth that matter to Zarathustra! Clearly, however, shall thine eye show unto me: free for what?
>
> Friedrich Nietzsche[5]

WE SPENT THE LAST CHAPTER trying to acknowledge that, here in our country, we've made the mistake of deifying certain experimental social policies, elevating them to a level nothing short of religious; and in doing so we have allowed these principles to demand of us the same unquestioned obedience as religious doctrine. One of these immortal principles, which will serve as a convenient illustration, is *Freedom*.

If you know one thing about yourself, you know that you are "free"—freer than any man before, supposedly. But freedom is

5. Friedrich Nietzsche, *Thus Spoke Zarathustra* (Blacksburg: Thrifty Books, 2009), 58.

not just a fact to be lived without a care. It isn't something you can just "have" without giving anything back. Freedom is a question. In fact, it is *the* question of human existence, which every person can feel weighing on him and which each must answer in some way or another, or else pay the consequences.

The more substantial the freedom exercised by a person, the more substantial the answer must be. This is why men of old did not rush so quickly into absolute liberty. They knew they'd have to come up with an absolute answer to this absolute freedom—and they knew that it would destroy them.

Liberate yourself too far and it comes rushing back at you like a boomerang or a tidal wave. It grips you around the neck, lifts you off your feet, and pins you against the wall, demanding an answer to the eternal question: "Free for what?"

But that's you, my dear liberated reader. You're free, just as everyone keeps telling you—but do you have an answer for that freedom? You know what you are free *from*, but do you know what you are free *for*? You don't—you can't. That's another thing that was destroyed when true tradition was wiped from the world. Tradition was the collective answer to a question no man could answer alone, but it is lost. Everyone became free to be whatever and whomever he wanted to be. We're all completely responsible for our own being and our own personalities. That's our great privilege, with no traditions and no real culture to speak of. And that's the Sphinx we feel standing over us, waiting to devour us lest we answer rightly.

How does this Sphinx-freedom feel to you? It has felt to me like a vacuum into which I was born and to which I cannot offer a justification. It feels like being freed into outer space, where freedom reigns infinitely, where you will find freedom and freedom only, in a chaotic emptiness.

Man at one time may have been born into a mold, and that mold may or may not have suited his preferences and talents. But you and I, we are born into a void—the molds were thrown out the window one and all! And a cold void suits nobody's fancy. I'm not saying I'd prefer a mold, necessarily. I can't be certain what I'd prefer, and that's the problem.

I'm told that I should design my "self" according to my desires, but how can I design myself unless I already know myself? It is a chicken-and-egg conundrum and I'm stuck in it. I don't think I have it in me to become wholly responsible for my own being and personality. No one does. I can contribute to the affair, and I would happily do so. I can discipline myself and I can work; I can learn and form my mind; I can enter relationships that impact me to the core and help me grow. But this is not enough. My parents contributed as well, but I'm still more than what they formed through their blood, sweat, and tears.

I'm beyond myself and doomed to live beside myself, alienated from my own person. This great and subtle thing, this Self, that has been tossed in my lap for me to play with is too powerful for me to develop alone and outside any supporting framework. I desire community, cooperation, companionship, direction, and the well-beaten paths, all multicolored and multifaceted, that these things provided in traditional civilizations.

As much as my culture taught me otherwise, *I need other people* to help me build my "I."

This new freedom is far too much responsibility, and it causes me more pain each time I'm reminded of how absolutely free I really am. I'm too much for me to handle alone. And that's what this freedom really is—it is a sentence of aloneness. My freedom is an exile. Regardless of what it was meant to be in the beginning, that's what it has become. It has removed man's connection to man, and now no one believes his fate is intertwined with any other living thing.

There's another lie I need to mention. It is the lie that says God once denied man freedom, and now that we have it we've delivered ourselves from God, we've escaped His arbitrary limitations. That, dear reader, is just another superstition modern people use to comfort themselves in an attempt to live with the freedom they can't answer for. They confuse the monster breathing down their necks with God. They think it's Him back there, but they are mistaken. No God ever ruled man's every move, threatening him with wrath at each step. The God of traditional religions left man free—all too free, it seems.

As for man's part, he was smart enough to understand the implications of this freedom and to build a framework of limitations around himself. The Greeks, as we all know, were obsessed with this moderation, and nothing offended them more than excess. They sensed the profound danger of exercising too far man's capacities. Some limitations are blessings—they are like iron bars of safety over a treacherous bridge. You can free yourself of them, but only a suicidal man would free himself from the things that sustain him.

When our forefathers liberated themselves and made "freedom" an absolute, they struck down all forms of safety and said: "Every man for himself!"

That's what happened when freedom—or "Liberty" as it is called—became an ideal held religiously by our civil religion. Your forefathers wanted to be free, and were allowed to become so. The consequences may have proven more than we can handle.

It was as if humanity liberated itself from its own sustaining atmosphere—all the spiritual air and cultural beauty got sucked right out from around them, even if it took a couple hundred years for people to feel the breech in the hull. Now everything is gone out into the void: community, wisdom, tradition, and limitation. Now our existence feels like a desert in which we are absolutely free, because although we can go anywhere we want, there is nowhere we really want to go to, and so we are not really free.

Now we're left under the weight of that great question: "Free for what?" All the principles for which men used to live and die are gone and all of the answers have gone with them. Free for what, then? That's what you have to answer, my dear reader. That's our task. We are floating in space, freer than free, and now we have to figure out some way to build around ourselves a cockpit. If we can, then maybe someday we can fly it back to earth and become human again—maybe even start a family.

Our job is to find the answer to our freedom. We need each other to find it, don't forget. We have to reach out and set our own limits again. It is only within the context of fixed limits that you can reach out and touch anything. You can't walk across the room unless you have a floor to push against with your feet. We crave the ability to walk around, and to touch and know one another. We've got to construct limits. Then perhaps you can finally find a *Self*—that deep identity which we have been told to build arbitrarily as if it were a pile of Play-Doh.

You can't build your own *being*. That was the great prideful absurdity of the whole affair. You can't do it. You can only *discover* your being, and it often takes a lifetime to find it.

That must be the new orientation and aim of human liberty: to know thyself—the Self which you do not build but were born with. Then, perhaps, you can answer the question, and only then can you safely and confidently take a little piece of your freedom, living not just free, but *free for this.*

Self-Consciousness

> The century...has been marked by the idea of 'modernism'—a self-consciousness new among centuries, a consciousness of being new...a sensation of anxiety and shame whose center cannot be located and therefore cannot be placated; a sense of an infinite difficulty within things, impeding every step; a sensitivity acute beyond usefulness, as if the nervous system, flayed of its old hide of social usage and religious belief, must record every touch as pain.
>
> John Updike[6]

Do you know what your problem is? You are self-conscious. By this I do not mean "selfish," as the moralists would say, but

6. John Updike, Foreword to *Franz Kafka: The Complete Stories* (New York: Schocken Books, 1971), ix.

something more like an inescapable, existential self-centeredness.

In this sense, we are quite possibly the most self-conscious people ever to walk the face of the earth. Remember the old story about Adam and Eve? That message is more about self-consciousness than anything else. When Adam ate the apple he moved from simply *being* himself to *thinking about* himself. He was ripped from living in comfortable unison with his identity—a unison so absolute that he never had to think about himself in the least—and was cast into the exile of his own head. Eden was his rootedness and his security, and his banishment was to the changeable, frail environment of his rational mind. When this happened, his existence was degraded one step, by which we say that he became "self-conscious."

That was the Fall that you've heard too much about. It was, ironically, a fall *up* into the mind and into the horrible insecurity of having to think about yourself in order to be reassured that you exist.

Now do you understand why they say that *death entered the world* at the Fall? Well, that only makes sense. If a man is not self-conscious, then death does not exist. You have to be concerned with the past and fearful for the future in order for death to threaten you. And it always threatens your Self, that thing which previously you weren't much concerned with. That's why the birds and the bees don't know death. They aren't self-conscious.

Adam ate the apple, it went to his head, and now he knows death. That's the knowledge he gained. That's the Fall, and man hasn't stopped falling since. Every step of the way he seems to become more and more trapped in his own head, more and more concerned with the precariousness of his Self and its existence.

In short, you are suffering from indigestion.

Whether or not you are Christian, and even if you don't take the story to be historical,[7] it certainly explains a lot. That's the only thing myths were ever meant to do anyway: they explain us to ourselves. And the myth of Adam explains you and me to a T. Why should we care if it happened at a specific place and time?—it happens every day within us. We know the Fall even if we don't know anything about God.

But as I was saying, it seems we cannot for one moment stop thinking about ourselves. Just listen to our music. Every hit song smacks of this particular form of insecurity, stuffed with lyrics demanding "acceptance for who I am" or "who we are," heaping praises on ourselves simply for "where we're from," never concerned with whether or not we've ever done anything worthwhile. That isn't arrogance, dear reader. It is self-consciousness. Whether you listen to country or gangster rap, the lyrics are always the same: it always amounts to a long string of self-congratulations for driving a big truck or a Cadillac, for being born in Dixie or the projects, for drinking Jack Daniels or Grey Goose, and always and everywhere for having indiscriminate sex.

7. The insistence on interpreting scriptures in their most literal sense is a modern phenomenon. Traditional Christianity never felt it necessary to claim that everything in the Old Testament was a literal-historical event.

The message at the bottom is always the same. It is a desperate and usually obnoxious attempt at self-assurance. That's why we drink it up—we can't get enough of these lyrics that praise us and convince us that we do indeed have some sort of worthwhile identity. Tune in to any radio station that plays the current "hits." What you will hear are the laments of self-alienated and self-conscious individuals. That is the artistic expression of our generation.

Ironically, even contemporary religious or "worship" music is saturated with this. Everything centers on "me," "mine," and "my God." Gone is cautious supplication of the Old Testament psalmist who spoke always of God's people in the plural. Our generation only wants to hear about a Jesus who is our "personal savior."

The worship music is always about all God has given us and gives us and will certainly continue to give us. We cannot allow into our minds a single ounce of doubt about our worthiness or about the possibility that we might have a test to pass first. Our Jesus only wants to hold us and squeeze us and shower us with blessings.

Eventually one begins to wonder whether God is in fact being praised, rather than the one praising engaging in self-praise. Such is the worship of a self-conscious Christianity. And so it is with our agnostic generation that, even when we go to church, we are unable to find or maintain any real certainty about who we are and where we stand in the world.

We cannot find enough inner stability to even confidently say "I AM." You can't say that, can you? You can't say something as simple as "I AM." You can only say, "I don't know." That's Adam's apple sitting in your stomach. That is the kind of pernicious knowledge that came from the old tree.

We all know that it is possible to think too much. Thought can drive you insane if you aren't careful. Sometimes thought can paralyze and destroy. That's our problem. You have to be rooted in your being before you start thinking. Rootedness and being must always come first or else your reasoning is tainted and undermined from the start. That's why our thinking, and the thinking of men in general for a long time now, is undermined and chaotic. All we have is the mind to cling to, and it doesn't work very well on its own. Anything can be rationalized, and if anything, then nothing.

Because we are rootless and disoriented, we start at the wrong end and reverse the process. We start at the wrong spot—in the head—and then try to arrive at our being. You must understand the great tragedy of this reversal and the story it tells. It is the essence of self alienation.

Have I lost you?

Consider the great motto of the rational age, which everyone has heard: "Cogito, ergo sum" (I think, therefore I am). Can't you see that this is completely and catastrophically backward? René Descartes, the man who said it, was doing what we now do habitually. In that regard, he was the spiritual father of us all. He was trying to find himself by starting with his own thoughts. Do you see that? He began in his thoughts, and by doing so he reduced the cosmos to a thought about the cosmos. He reduced his very existence to a thought about his existence. His very Self, the thing every man searches for his whole life, became nothing more than a thought about himself. "I think, therefore I am" is the motto of estrangement.

You are more than your own thoughts about yourself. I am more than a simple thought about myself. I may not know what exactly I am, but at least I know that I am not my own thoughts. That fatal "cogito" has become the unconscious maxim of our era and the heart of our crisis of self-consciousness.

At this point we should ask why the problem has become exaggerated for our generation. "Hasn't every other generation struggled with the same problem?" But the answer is "no." Our existential human condition has been modified, and so we are not like others before us. Our struggles carry the accent of our era.

We've already hinted at the problem. We observed that in the last few centuries mankind systematically carried out a revolution and rejected everything that came before. Man cut his traditional tether. He became what you and I call "modern."

Don't worry: this is not a treatise dedicated entirely to lamenting the "evils of the modern world." However, we do have to admit that the old social framework did at least help a man decide who he was and where he stood in regard to the universe. For example, there has always been religion, whatever form that religion happened to take. Religion explains much to man. It gives him rootedness and reassurance. It gives him a truth to hold to and around which to pivot. But the modern world has no religion, at least not in any real social or existential sense. Our religion is a private affair, usually more of a hobby, something "on the side," carried out as a social event for "fellowship," which pretty much renders it culturally inert.

We are individuals now. Individualism is an "American tradition," is it not? This means that most of the questions a civilization used to answer together, as a sort of collective, cooperative effort, are now each man's own battle to fight alone. Everything is a solo mission, and it has ended in tragedy.

Stripped of all the old structures and safe paths, we tend to wander through life unprotected. We are like bare wires, stripped of all insulating layers of culture and community and religion, spiritually naked and exposed, ready to short out at the slightest disturbance. *We are sensitive beyond all usefulness.* This disease of self-consciousness, then, is in a way uniquely ours.

The Verbal Universe

> My grandmother, who lived in a Moravian village, still knew everything through her own experience: how bread is baked, how a house is built, how a pig is slaughtered and the meat smoked, what quilts are made of, what the priest and the schoolteacher think about the world; she met the whole village every day and knew how many murders were committed in the country over the last ten years; she had, so to speak, personal control over reality, and nobody could fool her by maintaining that Moravian agriculture was thriving when people at home had nothing to eat. My Paris neighbor spends his time at an office, where he sits for eight hours facing an office colleague, then he sits in his car and drives home, turns on the TV, and when the announcer informs him that in the latest public opinion poll the majority of Frenchmen voted their country the saf-

> est in Europe (I recently read such a report), he is overjoyed and opens a bottle of champagne without ever learning that three thefts and two murders were committed on his street that very day.
>
> Milan Kundera[8]

MOST PEOPLE IN OUR COUNTRY live in the abstract. What I mean is that they don't judge the world by what they see happening or by their own experience, or even by their own judgment. In this freest of all democracies, men paradoxically depend more than ever before on distant and alien sources for their opinions. If we want to know how the country is doing, where it is going, who is going to be president, who is killing, who is being killed, what sort of laws are being changed, etc., we turn on the television or the computer and take what information we can find. We have no choice, of course. Our reality is far too complex for any one person to grasp in any comprehensive manner. The individual can only pull bits and pieces from the wires as the information flies by, and hope that what he grabbed was accurate.

This has some strange effects on our perception of reality. It tends to turn things upside down. For example, isn't it odd that everyone hears all about the president every single election, but few could name the members of their own city council? That's democracy working in the reverse, in its most ineffective manner—everyone paying attention to the one vote that they are least competent to cast, and completely disregarding the elements of their democracy that actually touch them and on which they'd be competent to decide.

8. Milan Kundera, *Immortality* (New York: HarperCollins, 1999), 212.

Yet this will appear normal to the voter simply because the television is clamoring all day about the distant caricature running for president, reinforcing the impression that the presidency is the one vote that matters. In comparison to this display, he'd have to spend a great deal of energy to actually meet his local representatives, who never appear on TV and so might as well not even exist. In this way his perception, not only of his own competence, but of his own ability to become competent, is reversed and exaggerated. He ends up ignoring the area of his activity where he could have maximized his impact, focusing instead with utmost intensity on those things which concern him least.

I have used politics here as a simple example, but this distortion of reality applies to our general perception of the world. We'll miss a local school board meeting that could affect local children because we are too busy watching a hostage situation taking place in a school clear across the country. We will see the distant crisis as more "important," and we are right in a way, but the crisis is not important in the sense that he can do anything about it. It is tragic, but it is also not our responsibility because it is out of our reach, regardless of how long we sit glued to the television watching it.

This is how it goes with every tragedy, every disaster, every war, and every new disease. Always the death tolls parading across the screen. Death is real, of course, and the ability to cope with death is important. But the disturbing carnage we see on the news does not give us a healthy, reasonable exposure to death—television only showcases death in its most fearful or anxiety-inducing forms. It sensationalizes death in such a way that it actually inhibits people from coping with it.

Real death that actually affects most of us—the kind we need to know about and experience in a healthy way—then becomes overwhelmed by all the tragedy on the television. Our concept of death becomes distorted and destroyed because of this exposure to things that have nothing to do with the parts of reality we actually touch.

This process deeply impacts us. It forms and informs us when we expose ourselves to it, and we are always being exposed to it. Our "information age" rips us from our immediate reality and forces us to become involved and concerned with a reality that is real but is not ours. We then begin to think, act, and even communicate with one another in accordance with that false reality.

This counterfeit reality is what I will call the *verbal universe*. It is an abstract world made of ideas and words and prejudices; and it is, I believe, a development particular to large, technologically developed societies. It is born of complexity because complexity overwhelms the individual by piling more information on his plate than he can possibly digest. This is exacerbated within democracies, because in a democracy a man is expected to have an opinion on everything, from the causes of cancer to the side-effects of vaccination to who is in the Super Bowl. It doesn't matter that he is truly incompetent in regard to many, if not all, of these things. It doesn't matter that even experts are often unsure about them, and that he, working full-time on a production line or in a grocery store, could not possibly know any better. He simply must have an opinion on every issue, every candidate, and every subject; and that is that.

Enter the verbal universe. The verbal universe provides an alternative to that impossible expectation of competence by instead providing the illusion of its fruition. The verbal universe offers the man an array of neatly packaged opinions; it offers him an answer to everything; and it offers him a common language—a specific set of keywords and phrases—through which he can then communicate his new opinions with others, so long as they also received their opinions from the same source. By this I do not mean that their opinions have to be exactly the same. They may very well be contradictory opinions, but the communication still succeeds so long as they both participate in the common verbal universe with its common language. Two men may hold opposite opinions, having selected very different "packages" from their source, but they can still speak to one another thanks to the common language, and that is what matters most, because successful communication is what provides the feeling of human potency.

Now the first thing you should notice about this verbal universe is the fact that it does not help people think or "know" in any meaningful way. In fact the whole reason it develops is that people do not have the time or aptitude to think. The keywords of the verbal universe, then, are simply tools to facilitate opinion-formation, enabling two people to debate a given issue, even with great vigor and passion, yet without really thinking about their premises at all; and, what's more, this enables men to "communicate" without having to consider what their opponent is saying either. Communication, within the verbal universe, is not communication: it is something more like a transaction or an exchange of mechanical responses and clichés. It has lost the human element.

A communicant does not have to meet any other person; communicants simply have to go through the ritual in which they compare keywords and opinion packages and either find themselves in perfect conformity or find their packages incompatible. If incompatible, each will deploy a second set of phrases, clichés, and pseudo-arguments to demonstrate that his combination is better, and that his "opinion outlet" is superior. Neither person need ever really hear what the other is saying. They only need to go through the motions. The communicants are then enabled to converse in a way that gives the *appearance* of meaningful communication, but both are talking without speaking, and hearing without listening.

This sort of quasi-communication survives and thrives for a variety of reasons, two of which we've already mentioned. First, it is an easy solution to the impossible problem of *competence in everything*. Second, once a certain verbal universe is adopted, it flatters the participant beyond all reason, thus reinforcing the illusion of universal competence. Once a man is convinced that he is capable of judging any matter, no matter how complex, for himself, then not only will he be dependent on the verbal universe for its comfort, but he will also become completely impervious to any doubt about his opinions once they have been adopted.

However, there is a third and final aspect of this universe which has helped it to overwhelm the entire modern world, and that is its efficiency. The verbal universe is able to accumulate and disperse information much quicker than reality itself ever could. And in a world which almost instinctively prefers the fast over the slow, the verbal universe wins out nearly automatically. The real world is always too slow, steady, and patient.

I hope I am not overwhelming you, dear reader. We'll move forward presently, but I want to clarify a couple of things in summary.

Keywords, slogans, catchphrases, and clichés: these are the tools of the verbal universe. They are its power, and you can use them to recognize its work. Its language consists of vague, common words, usually almost meaningless in themselves but in the verbal universe loaded with meanings. Think of "love," "hate," "democracy," "education," "sexuality," "patriotism," "freedom," "liberal," "conservative," and so on. Even the word "American" has the power to convey massive amounts of emotion, even if, in actual context, it means something else, or indeed nothing at all. These are the central tools utilized by the verbal universe to offer each person the ability to *communicate without communicating* and to *think without knowing*. And almost always the thinking and the speaking are about events which have nothing to do with the person.

As you learn to recognize this false reality, you'll find that it is paradoxical, because those who use it can communicate with anyone anywhere. Listen to two men on the street talking politics, parroting what was on the news that day. They go through a grand ritual, do they not?—either patting each other on the back or facing off as mortal enemies. And yet if you stopped them midstream and inserted some strange notion, something off the beaten path, they'd look at you as if you were speaking an entirely different language. And that's because you are. You are an alien, because you are not from their universe. That's the conundrum. If you really want to communicate, you'll have to accept the fact that real communication is difficult and that real subjects are complex. If you want to avoid impoverished, mechanical cliché-dialogue, then you may have to feel like the idiot in the room.

Alright: I know this chapter was a bit off in the clouds. We'll return to earth as we move forward, so long as you remember the existence of the verbal universe. It is everywhere, superimposing itself on the actual world and, very often, obscuring it from view completely. Peel it back, now, and see what is underneath. The real thing will never cease to surprise you. That's another way you can recognize the verbal universe: it always gives men exactly what they expect. That is its comfort and its lie.

Relationships

> Beshrew your eyes,
> They have o'erlook'd me and divided me,
> One half of me is yours, the other half yours,—
> Mine own I would say: but if mine then yours,
> And so all yours.
> Portia to Bassanio, *The Merchant of Venice*[9]

AH, RELATIONSHIPS. You'd think they were everywhere, listening to us talk. But there is no such thing as a "relationship," not really. Not in actuality. There are friends, comrades, cohorts, enemies, craftsmen, bosses, parents, siblings, lovers, wives, and husbands. But there is no such thing as a generic, neutral "relationship." The fact that today we use the term to apply to all interactions indiscriminately should tell us something about ourselves.

9. William Shakespeare, *The Merchant of Venice*, Act 3, Scene 2.

What does it tell us? It tells us that we are so agnostic that we recoil from attributing any qualitative character to our personal interactions. That's why we use the word "relationship." Do you have a new love interest? You aren't going to call it that, are you? You aren't going to call it a romance, a courtship, or even a new seduction. That's far too much commitment for you. You're going to call it a new *relationship*. That's our depth—that's as far as we are prepared to go. We won't even call our dates by that name. We say we are "hanging out." That term fits us better because it maintains our agnosticism about the situation.

The generic and empty word "relationship" signifies, at best, a neutral exchange or an agreement between two autonomous parties. It does not imply anything about the participants, in and of itself. It is a business term pertaining to purely *external* things, something a race of traders would bandy around. That's us, though, isn't it? We're spiritual barterers, traders of friendships, hagglers of love. We peddle our own wares and handle the wares of others as commodities, trying to get the best deal, leaving the rest, sometimes splurging if we feel courageous or lonely, but always careful, always cautious not to go beyond the level of a mere "relationship."

A relationship is a colorless, vacant monstrosity. It is evil not because of what it is, because it is really nothing; it is evil because of what it excludes. It is not an excess, it is a negation. It harms us not by leading us to an extreme, but by putting a perverse limit on our souls, inducing an inner atrophy.

In the way we use it, the term excludes the possibility of giving oneself for nothing. A relationship always implies two-way traffic. Two-way traffic isn't bad, by any means. Two-way traffic is the ideal. When I give love I'd like to receive love; when I come to the aid of a friend I'd like to think that he'd come to mine. But I can't know ahead of time that my love and aid will be reciprocated. I can't know that I'll be repaid in my friendships. If I knew, or demanded to know ahead of time, then it wouldn't be a friendship and it wouldn't be love. It would be a relationship. Relationships exclude love.

Relationships are safe. That's probably the main reason we adopted them, you and I and our generation. We were born into a sexually liberated world where everyone is personally atomized, alone, trustless. We were born in a time when something like life-long marriage sounded almost inconceivable. That's why we don't often have marriages. They are simply too risky. We don't have friendships either. They take too much time. We have *relationships* in which we know the cost and in which we can control the level of commitment, which is always a minimum.

No one can really blame you for using this lens to view the world, dear reader. You came into a society where community is a ridiculous notion. The Andy Griffith show isn't quaint for you—it's stupid. Naive to an extreme. The picture it paints is so far from your reality that you cannot even indulge in the playful exaggerations. You don't see the humor. *You don't have the capacity for nostalgia to which shows like that were made to appeal.* You can't imagine a community in which everyone is either friend or neighbor, where you are intimate with everyone even if it is only because you know of their vices and they know of yours. This is the world of "relationships."

We'll have to change that, you and I. We'll have to start taking risks at some point. At some point we'll have to leave the safety of the relationship behind. We'll have to rediscover the concept of sacrifice. That is something we could sink our teeth into, is it not? "Greater love hath no man..." and all that stuff. That's where the fire is.

Obviously neither of us wants to die for a friend or for love, but we can and should want the possibility to at least be open to us. If not, what will you do when, some day, you find yourself so rapt in affection for another human being that you feel inclined to make a sacrifice or take the bullet? In order to open that possibility we have to open ourselves again to love in its greatest extent, and this requires the rejection of relationships.

You'll have to go further than just changing your language, but using the right language truly is a start. You'll find it difficult enough just to apply qualitative terms instead of neutral ones. You'll have to call a date a date. That'll torture some of you beyond belief. You'll have to make investments of yourself that you know will have little to no return.

Risks—real risks! That's where the pain is, but that's where the depth of human feeling lies as well. That's where your humanity is hiding. Relationships are sterile. Bring back the life. The dirt and grime will come too, but oh, the beauty of life!—it's worth a bit of dirt here and there.

Sex

> Seeking to 'free' sexual love from its old communal restraints, we have 'freed' it also from its meaning, its responsibility, and its exaltation. And we have made it more dangerous. 'Sexual

> liberation' is as much a fraud and as great a failure as the 'peaceful atom.' We are now living in a sexual atmosphere so polluted and embittered that women must look on virtually any man as a potential assailant, and a man must look on virtually any woman as a potential accuser. . . . And in the midst of this acid rainfall of predation and recrimination, we presume to teach our young people that sex can be made 'safe'. . . . What a lie! Sex was never safe, and it is less safe now than it has ever been.
>
> Wendell Berry[10]

SOMETIMES, in our relationships, we have sex.

There is no such thing as "safe sex." The very phrase is not only a fiction but a contradiction in terms. It was a heinous crime to put that phrase into our heads. There is no such thing and there never was.

Some human things just aren't "clean." Some things are dangerous—both emotionally and physically—and often they cannot be cleansed without destroying the humanity of the thing itself. Sex is one act of that type; war is another. Making life and taking life cannot be sterilized without turning the whole affair into a monstrosity.

Look at war: the more our predecessors tried to remove man from the battlefield, from the invention of guns to the atom bomb, the more men died in each new battle. Comparatively few people died when men killed each other face to face, sword in hand; very few indeed, compared to those who died in their homes at Hiroshima, or those who died in their offices on 9/11.

10. Wendell Berry, *Sex, Economy, Freedom & Community* (New York: Pantheon, 1993), 142.

In every modern battle men die from bullets fired by men they have never even seen. Men die by the millions, all because our predecessors sought to remove man from the battle and make battle sterile. They pretended that by taking away the sword they had made war more "humane," but it is simply more monstrous than ever.

They did the same thing with sex. They tried to make it sterile and neutral, but they only succeeded in making it inhuman.

That is the concept of sex that we've inherited. They tried to tell us that it could be made "safe," and that we could control the transaction (and that's how it was taught to us, as a *transaction* within the context of a *relationship*). We were shown how it could be done carefully so that no negative consequences would follow. But sterilization means the destruction of all life. When you sterilize something, you don't just kill the harmful bacteria that was in it; you kill all the life that was in it. When we were given "safe sex," we were indoctrinated into a truncated sexuality, halted at the biological level before we fully understood even that elementary process.

We can now have safe sex. The success of our education is our curse. We can now "hook up" and complete the transaction without any repercussions, even the good ones. We avoid pregnancy, but also avoid the bond that comes from the self-giving part of coitus. We learned to get around self-giving and retain only the pleasure-getting.

The capacity to have sex and then walk away unfazed represents, in and of itself, a loss of feeling, a desensitization, and an impoverishment. The pain our educators thought they were teaching us to avoid was only one side of a coin; the other side was the apex of human communion. The man who can't feel the pain associated with sexuality—the man who can have "safe sex"—is the man for whom sex has lost the only thing that made it worthwhile. He has lost the fruit and is left holding only the rind.

Sex reduced to a process ensures that men and women will struggle to understand each other. Liberated sex, the sex of equality and neutrality, hides from us the fact that men and women always come to sex with different expectations and for different reasons. Thus, even when we do seek true communion we must fight to discard our blinders. We have to exert an immense effort just to see clearly again that we are different and that sex is not a clean affair. Furthermore—and this might be the hardest part—we'll have to acknowledge again that men and women are different, even if they are only different as the right and left hand are different. The right and left hand need each other if they are going to accomplish any meaningful work, or if they are going to make any beautiful music. Right now we don't know anything about right or left hands, and so we only get to hear the dull and awkward silence of one-hand clapping.

Marriage

WHERE RELATIONSHIPS AND SEX MEET, there some of us find marriage. This is the most foreign concept of all to our souls, besides religion, of course. Here we have to overcome our entire indoctrination, because everything is working against us. Consider the concept of the *relationship*. A man does not need a relationship with his wife. He does not need anything so abstract as that. He needs a woman—he needs *that* woman.

A married couple doesn't need all those books telling them how to focus on their "relationship" and keep it healthy and alive. They need to keep each other healthy and alive. They don't need to know how to feed this abstract thing, taking its temperature once a week on "date night," looking it over every morning to make sure it is okay and thriving.

A man needs to be a man—a whole man—and most men decide that in order to achieve that lofty goal, they need a woman. And not just any woman, not just a lover or a mistress, but *a wife*. Oh yes, dear reader, men *need* a woman to fulfill their calling. Not every man needs a woman, and not every man should get married, of course, but most men need one and so marriage is their path.

A husband and a wife do not have a relationship and don't need one. They should, in fact, stay as far from that as possible. What they need is each other. They are no longer autonomous parties in a transaction. If she dies he will go on, but it will be as a man who has been chopped in half at the waist.

Married people don't have relationships. Marriage doesn't happen in the abstract, connecting people through their brains and through an idea. Husbands and wives are connected organically and spiritually, which are actually one and the same connection. I have read quite a few marriage books. They all said almost exactly the same thing. They all spoke about nothing but the marriage relationship. So deeply have our lives become bogged down in the abstract that this has become the center of our marriage training—everything turns on "the relationship."

Through this reduction, marriage itself has been reduced to the status of something that must be maintained to ensure that both parties are getting something out of it, satisfied, fulfilled, and happy.

By abstracting marriage in that way you undermine it from the start. You take it with you into your head, where I have been warning you not to go. That's what our forefathers have done with marriage: they've put the marriage into the couple's heads. Putting a marriage in a person's head is suicide. Marriage should never exist in a person's head. Think of your closest friendships, when you had them, if you had them. Your friendship was not in your head. Perhaps it entered your head, but that was probably only when it was dying, or in a moment of superficiality on your part. In any case, it was rarely something you examined in your head as a "relationship." Friendships—true spiritual communions—are not in the head. So much more is marriage not, then, since it is so much more than a friendship!

But that's our generation, with our marriages in our heads, along with everything else. There, in the abstract, we read books about it, feed it, water it, and maintain it; and we undermine ourselves with every drop of water we feed the thing.

Get out of your head!—start living! Be a man or a husband, a woman or a wife! Don't think about it in the abstract, or if you must, do it only for the briefest of moments to check your steps.

Gender

An industrial society cannot exist unless it imposes certain unisex assumptions: the assumptions that both sexes are made for

> the same work, perceive the same reality, and have, with some minor cosmetic variations, the same needs.
>
> Ivan Illich[11]

MARRIAGE BRINGS US unavoidably to gender. The modern difficulty with gender throws into light perhaps the most intimate aspect of our self-doubt. We have applied our disbelief to our own sex! We can't even bring ourselves to say for certain whether a man is a man or a woman. It's all too final.

You have got to stop living in your head. I cannot say that enough. That was the worst thing our education did to us. It taught us to live in our heads first and in reality second. How much of our reality has been lost because we live in our heads!

Consider, for example, our starting point when we try to think about gender. We start, as usual, with a generic, neutral, and abstract thing called a "person." What is a "person"? Once again, there is in reality no such thing. This imaginary, abstract, sexless thing, devoid of personality and all intrinsic qualities, exists in our heads and nowhere else.

But that's where we start from, thanks to our exceptional habit of abstraction. We start from the sexless imaginary thing and then take reality into consideration: we apply a sex to it, as if that were a secondary matter of deciding which color shirt to wear. When we reason by this process, then no one is a man wholly and completely. There is no such thing as this type of man. There are only "persons" in a more or less masculine guise. That's how we wear our sex, as though it is not part of us, but simply something attached to us on the outside.

11. Ivan Illich, *Gender* (New York: Pantheon, 1982), 9.

Gender is not like that, dear reader. It is not something that exists only between the legs.

Your gender is something intrinsic to your being. It isn't a set of biological clothes applied as an afterthought, accidental to the rest of you. Your gender pierces you to your core. It defines you and colors everything you do and see. Men and women experience the world in entirely different ways, not just when they are standing naked in front of a mirror, but always.

When my gender defines my being and forms the framework of my life, then it is too close for me to hate or separate from myself. But what happens to us now that we perceive ourselves essentially as neutral "persons" without gender? What happens when it is only a set of clothes? It is entirely possible for me to feel uncomfortable in a set of clothes. I can outgrow my clothes. I can change style and taste. I can take off my clothes if I don't like them.

Once I begin to perceive something about myself as external to myself, it becomes "not myself." At that moment I can start resenting it and begin to feel it as an oppression. A man who experiences himself as a man pure and simple, and not as a "person who happens to be male," cannot resent his manhood. It would be an impossible conception, and if it were possible it wouldn't make any sense. It would be like resenting his being, which no person can do. A person can resent his life, because that takes place temporarily and externally. A man can even kill himself, but he cannot resent his being. That is why the man who does not see manhood as something "on the outside" also cannot imagine his manhood oppressing him in any way. It *is* him.

The same goes for women. Womanhood *is* the woman.

At least that's what reality tells us. It only sounds strange and makes us uncomfortable because we have gotten our sex into our heads, along with our relationships and the universe at large.

Now here we are with our manhood and womanhood in our heads, with gender beginning to feel like an *afterthought*. This also means that to call oneself a man or a woman feels like a decision and a commitment, which is universally terrifying to our agnostic natures.

It feels as though by calling myself a man I'm making a commitment to something and burning some bridges, forfeiting all the alternatives. It sounds like I'm agreeing to wear the same set of clothes the rest of my life and that's asking quite a bit. No one wants to do that. We are afraid of being "trapped" in our sex. Most of us don't struggle with this about ourselves, of course, but it is no exaggeration to say that we feel it about our neighbors. Even if we know what we are, we refuse to say of someone else: "He is a man." We'd hate to make a commitment for him and oppress him with his sex. We were taught about ourselves in the abstract, and now we cannot reconcile our ideas about ourselves with the reality that is *us*.

The hardest part about recovery is that the old supports are gone. Our parents had their sex in their heads as well. Now the landscape is a landscape for *persons* only. We built a civilization just for imaginary things. That is our heritage—that all the old pathways that allowed men to be men and women to be women are gone. All the old realities that corresponded to the insides of men and women are now only memories which we've been taught to hate and despise as "sexist." They are primitive, backward, dead, and gone.

We were taught to celebrate our liberation from these old limits. Remember that we inherited the void of liberty. It was a liberation from ourselves, because we are men and women. We aren't sexless *persons*.

Is it any wonder we men are now ashamed of our manhood?—that we live our lives uncertain of ourselves, often effeminate, weak, and passive? No woman really wants this in a man, and so we are unattractive. And a woman, for her part, only wants to be a woman; but we of our generation have been taught to resent that too. Men are taught to be ashamed of masculinity, and our women are taught to resent their femininity. "Equality," they call it—at least we've been "equal" in our self-alienation and confusion.

Now our women go around half-naked. Is that any surprise? Why shouldn't they? They are genderless and so they have nothing to hide. All that skin that's showing? Well, that's secondary. We are persons first, and that's what matters. All that flesh is just clothing. It shouldn't stir anything in the enlightened mind. But it does. And so we men are forced to live ashamed of what it stirs within us, which is to say, we are forced to be ashamed of being men and of having the natural response of masculine beings. Because we cannot escape it we end up objectifying these half-naked women. We don't like that, but we can't do anything about it.

You and I cannot bring our children into this sort of self-hate and agony. We'll have to build something new in the world. It won't be an entirely new world, in the sense that it might very well resemble the old world—the one we were taught to hate and berate as primitive. It won't be a copy of the old either, though. That isn't my goal.

I simply say that it must not be a world designed for *persons.* It will be a world designed around men and women. It will be a world where men and women can once again feel at home in their own skin, feeling it finally as theirs and not as something else foreign and unwelcome.

Our new civilization must reject the *person* that does not exist and never has. We have to create (or re-create) a gender-friendly civilization built around people as they really exist: a civilization based not on an abstract mental conception, but on a real truth about humanity.

Adulthood

> Deprive young people of a rite of passage into the social order and they will look for a rite of passage out of it.... The effect of current policies has been to subsidize out-of-wedlock births, to remake marriage as a contract of cohabitation, and to drive religion, which is the true guardian of rites of passage, from the public sphere. Those policies have been embarked on with the best of intentions, but with a remarkable indifference to what we know of human nature.
>
> Roger Scruton[12]

12. Roger Scruton, "Riots of Passage," *The American Spectator*, October 2011, accessed November 3, 2014, http://spectator.org/articles/36841/riots-passage.

What is adulthood? We have no idea, do we? All we know is that that's what we are—we are "adults."

At least in this particular area our society is as openly agnostic as we are. No one knows what adulthood means. So ignorant are we all on the subject that we decided to put in place a law to tell us who is and is not an adult. Age eighteen sounded about right. That's completely arbitrary, though, and we know it. That's why we continue to forbid so-called adults from doing things as simple as drinking alcohol. We feel the need to be cautious when dealing with this "adulthood" thing which is so elusive and mysterious to us.

It weighs on us, though, this ignorance about our state in life, always wondering whether we are boys, girls, men, women, or just hovering in some intermediate state. This is yet another entirely new problem, suffered by no civilization before us. And here again we can see the cause in the same poisonous root: abstraction. Here as everywhere else we have withdrawn into our heads to try to find security in a reality which has become absurd.

Remember that man is now a "person," and a person contains within it no real qualitative distinctions. In our agnosticism we gave up on that whole effort, the effort at making distinctions between things, because it terrified us. We cannot even say for certain if a person is a man or woman, remember? It only makes sense that, along with the loss of all our other certainties, we would lose our ability to distinguish between child and adult. That's just one more qualitative distinction, and it must go out the window with all the others, no matter how much we need it. And we need it badly.

Everyone needs to know where he stands in life. He needs to be provided with methods and instruction through which he can learn to align his inner world with the world outside of him, teaching him how to deal with the struggles that will inevitably weigh upon him in that world.

What good does it do a man if an external law says to him: "Happy birthday! You turned a certain age and now you are a man!" This tells him nothing about himself, only about exterior things. It tells him that the world will now treat him differently; but it does not in any way explain to him how he himself has changed, how he has suddenly become adequate to these new circumstances, and why he should now be expected to meet what, the day before, was considered too great a burden for him to shoulder. A dramatically new degree of accountability is simply applied externally to a "person" who may or may not have graduated to a higher state of being.

Any hint that a particular youth may not be equipped for the task automatically registers as shame and is met with disdain. If you aren't ready, you only have yourself to blame—that's what we're told.

Oh, how our elders love to say: "You are eighteen! You are a man now! Act like it!"
"Act like what?"—we respond.
"You know . . . like *tha* . . . like a man!"

And it is at that moment that we realize they do not know the answer either.

It has been said that "indignation is the soul's defense against the wound of doubt about its own."[13] By making our elders conscious of their own ignorance on this subject we ignite indignation, for which we must suffer the consequences.

The same goes for women, though of course in a different way. Regardless of gender, then, the message is clear: adulthood is something that is supposed to occur naturally and automatically, with no special affirmation, intervention, or graduation. According to our civilization, adulthood is not something to be *facilitated*; it is only something to be acknowledged legally for the sake of categorization and social organization.

To begin to understand this crisis, we must again speak of individualism. If we do not understand this existential, spiritual, and psychological plague, we will make no progress. Here, in the realm of human development, the contemporary man suffers most acutely and obviously its repercussions; here individualism undermines entire generations and brings civilization itself to a halt.

The problem is one of deprivation. That's what individualism is: it is a deprivation of cooperation, proper peer relations, and cultural supports. Individualism suffocates the process of spiritual and mental growth by limiting each to what he himself brings to the table, which is never very much. It works the same for entire generations.

Let us examine the process broadly:

In order for a generation to successfully achieve the transition

13. Allan Bloom, *The Closing of the American Mind* (New York: Simon and Schuster, 1987), 71.

from childhood to adulthood—in order to make that qualitative leap—three things are required: 1) a supporting and reinforcing culture, 2) a group of caring, experienced elders to guide the way, and 3) the empathy and companionship of one's peers.

These three requirements must all be present within the actual context of graduation into adulthood. That they exist *generally* in a society is irrelevant.

So first, in regard to culture, each generation needs a specific and colorful framework in which it may develop, mature, and take advantage of guidance as it grapples with maturity. Because of our deep and near-universal mentality of individualism, this aspect of the "coming of age" process is totally non-existent.

In an individualistic society each man's fate is entirely in his own hands. No one owes him anything; but more than that, there is an almost mystical belief that, even if someone wanted to help his neighbor with some great personal struggle, he couldn't do it. It's as if we believe we can't touch each other in that way, even if we wanted to.

Thus, in regard to the would-be man, his neighbors are not only absolved of any assistance they traditionally may have owed him in the journey, but he is also made very aware that he should never have needed their assistance in the first place. We say that the young man should be able to transform himself from child to adult entirely without any beaten path designed specifically to achieve that purpose. You, dear reader, are left to your own devices.

Without culture, the remaining two requirements (the guidance of elders and companionship of peers) naturally fall apart. They rested on the first.

The elders forget that it was ever their job to lead the young at the moment of transition. They were once given this task consciously and with great fanfare. Each year they proudly led the graduates across the intimidating and precarious abyss between childhood and adulthood. It wasn't just for fun and ceremony. Their guidance was considered vital, and their experience was life-saving.

But what's more, and perhaps what is even more foreign to our mentality, is that their *acknowledgment* was also vital. They not only must guide the young across the bridge, but also must stand with them on the other side and affirm their success. Adulthood was a credential, and it came from other adults, not from any abstract law.

Today, because the elders believe that adulthood just "comes" at a certain age, they can only express surprise, frustration, and anger at the fact that it never comes. They blame the youth exclusively, not knowing that their own absence and condemnation is a profoundly undermining force behind the failure.

This also creates the problem of "surrogate initiations." Beneath all the individualistic rationalization, there still exists among parents a strong desire to see their children become adults. Even though their individualistic mentality denies their ability to facilitate such a transition, it persists nonetheless. Because it persists, it sooner or later finds unconscious expression in dangerous ways, such as when "recreational activities" like youth sports are given a shamefully exaggerated importance in the social life. You see, we cannot help but acknowledge that there is something in this *struggle for victory over some obstacle* that is good for young people, but because we don't know exactly what we are admiring, we fail to see the obvious: that an infatuation with "sports" cannot get the job done.

Moving now to the third requirement, which is peer support, we can see that, lacking both a social framework and a group of wise guides, each generation remains atomized and estranged, seeking something but unsure of what it seeks. Camaraderie of the young evaporates. We can no longer cling to each other as we endure the vicissitudes of "growing up." We are individuals. We cannot empathize even with those closest to our condition.

Here surrogate initiations enter the picture once again. Resourceful as young people tend to be, and feeling in their depths the need for a dramatic transition—something more experiential than some abstract legal acknowledgment—they develop new "rites" and attempt to force themselves, often violently, through these rites and into adulthood.

What was once a community affair, planned and conducted with purpose and within conditions of relative safety, guided by the wise and shared with one's fellows, now takes place willy-nilly and in the dark.

Sex, for example, is probably the most widely utilized surrogate initiation. In fact, phrases like "rite of passage" and "coming of age" almost automatically make the modern mind go to sex. That is because these phrases have taken on an exclusively sexual connotation.

We see every day the results of the "sex right"—this unconscious sex initiation—through the problems of sexually transmitted diseases, teen pregnancies, unwed mothers, and absentee or irresponsible fathers. To this the elders have reacted with typical blind futility, trying to remedy the problem by teaching a purely physiological kind of sex to children in school.

We already know the results of that sort of "sex ed." Without taking into account all the non-physical considerations involved in sex, the effort backfires. "Sex ed" creates a child who then goes forth eating the rind and discarding the fruit—missing the best parts of things and remaining empty. Rinds don't nourish. And so, after the failures of sex ed, we find abortion. That's what passes for progress today: solving human problems by destroying human life.

While the sex initiation does violence to both men and women, other surrogates seem to have greater impact on men. The reason for this is obvious. There is just something in the polarity of the masculine soul that seeks initiation almost violently. A man cannot rest without it. Man is the pioneer, after all. He is the warrior. He therefore must know when, how, and why he is a man, and he will have that affirmation one way or another.

Some men express this need in humorously obvious ways, such as driving a vehicle that is large or loud beyond all reason; some men, again, look to sex; some take an inordinate interest in sports or hunting; some take drugs; some get drunk; some get drunk and fight; some rebel; most find some odd combination of all these. Street gangs and their infamous pseudo-initiations are nothing but a very obvious and aggressive expression of this need, writ large for us to stare at wide-eyed and aghast. We must not lie to ourselves and think that simply because "gang beatings" are extreme they are incongruous with the times.

The biggest difficulty with all these surrogate initiations is that they are sought and acted out unconsciously. This means that they can neither serve their purpose nor be controlled within safe limits. They are just traumatic experiences sought in an effort to satisfy a valid desire, but doomed from the start to undermine the participant. They are truly counterproductive. Rather than leading to a stable adulthood, which is the goal, they preclude the possibility of its ever being attained. They lead to prison, single parenthood, injury, degradation, addiction, or death. They short-circuit an initially valid aspiration and drive one to self-destruction.

That is our situation: deprived of culture, abandoned by our guides, and isolated from our fellows, we travel alone. Most of us never reach the destination. We never cross that bridge into the land of men and women. It's as though someone forgot what the bridge was for, and so set it on fire. Now we just feel the cold air rushing out of the chasm and dream of what the other side must be like. We are not children, but neither do we feel like *whole men*, or *confident women*. We simply exist.

Children

> For a child is the very sign and sacrament of personal freedom. He is a fresh free will add to the wills of the world; he is something that his parents have freely chosen to produce and which they freely agree to protect. . . . He is a creation and a contribution; he is their own creative contribution to creation. . . . People who prefer the mechanical pleasures to such a miracle are

> jaded and enslaved. They are preferring the last, cooked, indirect, borrowed, repeated and exhausted things of our dying Capitalist civilization, to the reality which is the only rejuvenation of all civilization. It is they who are hugging the chains of their old slavery; it is the child who is ready for the new world.
>
> G.K. Chesterton[14]

WE'VE GOT TO BUILD a life-affirming civilization, and any life-affirming movement must begin by being a child-affirming movement. If your society can't welcome new life, then it can't possibly be friendly to the life that is already in it. Life-friendly is child-friendly. You can't pretend to have the former if you don't have the latter.

Today children are universally acknowledged as an inconvenience. No one even has to argue about it. Children are a burden and to have a child is to make a grand sacrifice. Those who decide to have children and those who don't will only differ on whether or not they decide that the reward is worth the cost.

"Should we? or should we not? Is the time right?" All the positives and negatives are weighed. Each couple must decide for themselves if they are "ready." And they are right, of course. It *is* a big decision and a grand sacrifice. That's the point. That's the heart of it—we have transformed the child from blessing to curse.

That is *in itself* the most anti-child aspect of our civilization—more than abortion and birth control and all those raging, passionate debates. Once you make children a burden, everything else just sort of falls into place.

14. G.K. Chesterton, "On Babies and Distributism," in *The Collected Works of G.K. Chesterton*, vol. 3 (San Francisco: Ignatius, 1990), 441.

So far has this trend progressed that we can't imagine any other arrangement or attitude. Yet we know that things weren't always this way. We know that children were once ardently desired by fathers. To be childless was to live in shame. For a woman, the greatest disgrace was to remain barren. Even long after the days of Abraham and Sarah, children were rushed into the world not by accident or for lack of condoms, but because they were an honor and an asset. They were not only prized, but actually useful.

Children in our world aren't useful. You and I were not brought into this world so that we could contribute. (That was the beginning of our spiritual undermining: we were purposeless from the start.) We weren't brought here for some great responsibility or so that we could take hold of an inheritance or to learn our father's trade. We were brought here as a sacrifice and a yoke.

We are most of us thankful for our existence, but we also can't help but resent the fact that we came here devoid of any real use to our parents beyond "emotional fulfillment." The emotional, you see, is only real for the feeler. It does nothing for the child. No one wants to be born for "emotional fulfillment." But that is the purpose of children and the deciding factor as to whether or not they enter the modern world.

Children are to be had or not depending on whether they will "fulfill" the parents. In this sense they are something like a dog or a cat, only more expensive. Religious factors may also come into play, but that often amounts to the same thing.

There's also something new and degrading in the attitude toward children as entirely optional and therefore unnatural.

Children are a "marriage accessory"—they don't come in the standard package but you can add one if you want. Just remember: it costs!

In large part, this is the fallout of artificial sterility. Such an attitude could not have come into being if it were not so incredibly easy to avoid what used to be the inevitable outcome of sex. In this way the child becomes something separate from marriage. Again, as before, we see a move from the real to the abstract. Now marriage is one decision, and the child is something else entirely. This shakes civilization to its foundations, because civilization was built on the assumption that the two things were inseparable.

Pregnancy, removed from its typical context and its normal place in a chain of events, becomes something to be manipulated. It becomes something we can adjust to fancy and whim, and its product, the child, inevitably shares this fate. Remember that now the child has become its own abstract decision, separate from the marriage decision. Once this point is reached in the process of abstraction, abortion naturally follows. The child was the result of a "choice," was it not? It is just a possibility, and we can prevent possibilities through technology and surgery.

Remember our shame? Do not think that this generalized child-hate has nothing to do with your condition. You were brought into this world useless, born a hardship. In fact you were lucky to have entered the world at all. Even if you were loved dearly by your parents—I know that I was—you were nonetheless also an affliction.

If we wish to eradicate our shame, we will have to find a way to reconstitute a child-friendly civilization. The point can't be ignored. I'm not sure how we'd start, exactly, but I'll leave you with one observation which suggests a possibility.

The factory worker, the man on shift-work, the man in the office, and the man taking orders at the burger joint cannot have any use for children. Even if he could bring a child into such a place, the child could not comprehend the work being done there. It would seem monstrous to him. Work has become something that a child can neither understand nor observe nor respect. This has deprived the child of very much, considering it was once the father from whom children learned almost everything.

A child could have once watched in awe as the father worked his trade; and the child, step by step, could have participated and someday become a fellow artist. This sort of active and developmental bond between father and child was a living, breathing thing. It not only made children useful, but made a relationship between father and child possible. Today this is only possible outside working hours, in the evening. And even if the child could go to a modern office, he would only be bored and confused watching the father talk on a phone or stare at a computer for eight hours straight. The child would not be in awe of the work he saw—he would be appalled. He would not want to grow to be like his father; he would want to avoid that at all costs.

I only dwell here on the modern interplay between work, child, and father to illustrate that our social structure has separated children from fathers and helped to render the former useless.

Any remedy must be multifaceted. If we want to reintegrate the child with the family and the world, we might have to reintegrate the father with the family. If we want to do that, we might have to change our assumptions about work itself.

It would obviously be a great evil to allow the child into the "workforce" as it is now. We tried sending children to factories once, and we know how that turned out. No, sending children to work, as work is currently arranged, will not benefit or fulfill the child. It doesn't even fulfill the father. We have to go in a different direction entirely.

I would never move the child toward the modern economy—but I would move the modern economy toward the child. Do you see the difference?

Everything runs together. All of our problems touch one another, and so our solutions will have to be far-reaching and intertwined. We can't make things better for the child without also making them better for men and women. The child, the family, work, art, education, and a better world will all have to come hand-in-hand, or they will not come at all.

Church

> We live in a land of WWJD bracelets, Jesus-is-my-homeboy t-shirts, Jesus-is-my-boyfriend music, and 'Tebowing.' We traverse a 'Christian' landscape as garish as a Thomas Kinkade painting, strolling to the beat of that sickly sweet poem about footprints. . . . The Bible is not a self-help book, and while the Gospel is indeed good news, the Evangelists were not cast in the mold of modern-day motivational speakers. Emotionally

> driven praise and worship songs are not going to win over anyone, and I swear, if one more person tries to tell me that the etymology of intimacy is 'into-me-see,' I'm going to have an aneurism.
>
> Michael W. Hannon[15]

Now that we've beaten a few existential problems into the ground, we had better move on to the larger institutional issues. First and foremost of these is the church.

You probably think that there isn't much to be said about church at this point. After all, we've spoken on and on about our disbelief—"What have we to do with church?" you ask. "Everything!" I answer. Our awkward relationship with religion is one of our most telling characteristics. By discussing it we can learn a great deal both about ourselves and about the state of Christianity in general.

But perhaps I should backtrack for a moment. I forgot to mention our virtue.

We have a virtue—I bet you didn't know that. We've spent so much time talking about our woes and our weaknesses that you probably didn't think we had a single admirable quality. We have one, though. It is our deep sensitivity to *hypocrisy*.

We loathe this particular form of dishonesty, and because of the strength of our hatred for hypocrisy, we are hypersensitive to all

15. Michael W. Hannon, "Would You Like Some Wine With That Cheese?," *Ethika Politika*, June 7, 2013, accessed November 3, 2014, http://ethikapolitika.org/2013/06/07/would-you-like-some-wine-with-that-cheese/.

forms of inauthenticity, be it religious, political, or otherwise. We can smell it a mile away like a shark smells blood. It only takes one drop of hypocritical blood in our ocean for us to detect it. If you've got deceit running through your veins you'd better stay out of the water. You know that I'm right, dear reader. And that's why we avoid churches.

You see, they are mistaken who think we keep our distance from churches because we don't care for spiritual depth, or because we are shallow, or because think ourselves "smarter" than religion. That is the opposite of the truth. Many of us have tried church. Many of us have poured ourselves into the worship that takes place within those walls. We summoned all our strength trying to "believe" and to be "born again" through that belief. It just didn't take. We weighed the whole thing and found it wanting. We tested the waters of the church, you might say, and we left the pool not because the water was too deep, but because it was too shallow.

Contemporary churches are saturated with two things that we cannot stand: procedure and sentimentality.

The traditional churches come off as a purely procedural affair, asking only a mindless and heartless participation in a weekly routine. It is common for people to accuse these churches of proclaiming a "salvation by works," but we know better. We've been there, and we did not see any salvation by "works." A salvation by works is something we might have been able to buy into. If we'd have found that we might have stayed. But we found something far lesser than works. We found "salvation by procedure"—and that is something we could not swallow.

Works are living and breathing—procedure is stultifying and dead. We are already immersed in procedure up to our necks. Our education was procedural, our work is procedural. We can't take any more.

And in the contemporary churches we find an equal but opposite superficiality. If the traditional varieties did what they knew without feeling, the contemporary churches do what they feel without thinking. Sentimentality reigns supreme in these modern services, and this too we find repugnant.

Remember that our strength is an acute sensitivity to the superficial and the inauthentic. Because of this we were able to pass judgment easily and immediately: there is simply not much for us within the contemporary religious culture.

Beyond all this, I'm sorry to say, is the contemporary Christian himself, or at least a certain type of contemporary Christian whom we all know. There are no doubt a great variety of beautiful people who live as Christians. That much is true. But there is one type who has come to predominate in our eyes, and who floods our view of "Christianity" each time we hear that word. Whether or not this specific "type" of Christian predominates in actual number, we cannot say. Maybe he just speaks the loudest, or gets out the most. All we know is that we are more familiar with him than any of the others. Thus, while acknowledging that there is surely a variety, we must deal with this one familiar type.

He is obnoxious, first of all. He seems to have developed a mental condition which I will call "proselytism mania." It drives him to "evangelize" us at all of the most inappropriate times, trying to share with us his truth. He is rude, in the sense that he presumes to know our most intimate depths before he even knows our names. Because of our hypersensitivity to superficiality and hypocrisy, he triggers in us the deepest resentment.

We see in his mentality a driving passion to convince us that he is right about something. He says that he is trying to introduce us to Jesus, our "personal savior," but our keen perceptions reveal to us a different truth: he is trying to introduce us to himself. He not only wants us to accept Christ into our hearts; he wants us to accept him. He needs us. Every man he can coax into being born again is an affirmation of his identity. The project in which he is engaged is evangelism, alright; but it is *evangelism in the reverse*. He is trying to bring us to "faith" so that he can rest in his.

We then come to a shocking realization: *the man obsessed with evangelism is just as much an agnostic as we are!* He is one of us, acting unconsciously and in a different guise. The Christian who *must* evangelize his friends is just like the pop music star who writes songs demanding self-affirmation. He is crying out for security in his identity because he does not have it.

The contemporary "Evangelical" movement is, to us, just another expression of our shared condition of self-doubt.

We are then told that to reject Christ is to accept damnation. That's the last resort. But we aren't rejecting Christ. We are rejecting the evangelist and his neediness, which is quite a different thing. He tried to sell us *his* Jesus and we didn't like the product. It left a nasty taste in our mouths. We'd be open to meeting Jesus, but we have the nagging conviction that he wouldn't go around handing out "WWJD" bracelets. We sense that this man's superficial version of Jesus is getting between us and Jesus. We react accordingly: by asking him to step aside.

We don't hate truth. We crave it. There is something we envy in the monk or the mystic. We envy their certainty and their peace. We don't think they are fools, we just can't find what they have and we refuse to pretend otherwise. We won't be hypocrites.

We want truth more than anything else. More than pop music, motivational speeches, and youth groups. We want to meet others authentically; that's why we don't want to go on Christian "mission" vacations where we'll be forced to impose ourselves on people we can't truly meet or understand. That is hypocrisy and we won't do it.

We don't want a shallow "Extreme Home Makeover" experience where everyone gets warm fuzzies and cries at the end. We don't mind crying, but only if the drama is real; we don't want that manufactured stuff just so that we can have a release. We don't want any part of that.

But that's what church feels like. It feels like a situation manufactured to give security, warm fuzzies, and emotional indulgence to a culture starved of true, deep, invasive feeling.

We don't want an anesthetic of naïveté and optimism. We want a church of life and virility and depth. We'll have a church of life or we won't have one at all. We won't accept this dose of "feel-good" just to offset the mechanical insanity of the daily grind. We want something so powerful it bleeds over and destroys the insanity. The fact that modern churches stay within the church and only come out during "ministry" time is proof of their impotence. We want something potent.

We do want salvation. We want salvation from our shame and our alienation, but we won't accept counterfeits. And we see counterfeits everywhere. We cannot but refuse what we feel to be less than true. That is our painful virtue. This is why we avoid churches and church-goers. We haven't rejected God. If we had then we would be atheists. But we aren't atheists, we are agnostics. We don't hate God. We don't hate Christianity or Christ. We just can't pretend we know them when we don't. We won't *trade our spiritual integrity for a mess of pottage*. We'd rather live in pain than live what would be to us a lie. *We refuse to blaspheme the holy spirit within us*. For that reason we abstain from church. Someday our abstinence may come to an end, accompanied with all the *rejoicing in heaven* that we've heard so much about. But not today. And probably not tomorrow.

Politics

> You went to vote bursting with enthusiasm, proud of your right to have a say. We can only laugh at your naïveté. None of us still believes today that he can change something with his vote. We only vote if there's nothing good on TV.
>
> Markus Willinger[16]

YOU DON'T VOTE WITH PASSION. In fact, you probably don't vote at all. For this you are said to be socially apathetic—a political deadbeat who prefers to leave his thinking and acting

16. Markus Willinger, *Generation Identity: A Declaration of War Against the '68ers* (London: Arktos, 2013), 23–24.

to others. The truth is precisely the opposite, though, isn't it? It is not that you don't care enough to vote. It's that you care enough not to vote. You've discerned the futility of the affair and you simply choose not to be patronized.

You've watched the presidency change hands every few years, and every time you have to endure the media and the party members propagandizing you, promising utopia if "their guy" wins, and assuring us that our civilization will collapse if "the enemy" is victorious. Well, you've seen both guys win a number of times, and it seems to you that civilization is still collapsing.

When it comes down to it, neither party is much interested in what you and I would call civilization—they are only interested in their victories and their control over the machinery. They want to be at the helm so they can steer, but we don't care for where they are steering. They aren't concerned with good government. American political life is not about governing and hasn't been for a long time. That's why we don't care much for the whole circus.

This isn't a "neutral" stance. We aren't "undecided." We are very much decided. We've just decided against both of the options before us.

We don't hate democracy. We just happen to believe that there is more to democracy than filling out ballots. We know that just getting to pick between two smiling millionaires on TV, neither of whom we know anything about, is not democracy—it is an insult. We don't feel privileged; we feel patronized.

Unless we have some say as to who appears on the ballot, then we really don't have any say at all. We'll consider voting when we've chosen what we're going to vote about and whom we're going to vote for. We've never felt like that. The fact that previous generations believed that their vote was their voice is something incomprehensible to us.

But the machine presses forward each year with greater fanfare, with campaigns so expensive that it is downright embarrassing, and men continue passionately following the drama. We don't believe politics is about self-government. Things have gone too haywire for anyone to believe that our democracy provides this function. It is all too far-removed from us and abstract.

We have come to know what it's really all about. It's about coping with the modern man's impotent and somewhat meaningless existence. Men are thwarted at every turn, kept spiritually inert and mentally anesthetized, glutted by all the basest of human pleasures; and because men feel the reality of their situation weighing upon them, they experience inner turmoil. They want so badly to act and to actually do something in the world besides watch TV and make more money. Democracy, the abstract notion of participating in the grand decisions of government, offers them that salvation, and they seize upon it. Democracy provides a promise—a promise of potency, self-assertion, and control in an undermined existence.

That's the political climate into which we were born. We cannot watch a political debate without feeling pain and we can't watch a State of the Union address without falling asleep.

We see nothing but a bunch of thwarted and angry men who crave an escape. For this escape they need only two things, an enemy and a savior—and that only requires two parties. That's why politics has degenerated into party politics, with the same two tribes warring year after year. If men were looking for a variety of options that they could sift through in order to select the truest and most prudent solution to a problem, they'd need several parties. If men wanted truly talented and timely leadership, they'd demand a variety of candidates and they'd find a way to extend the selection process beyond the rich and politically groomed. But they don't want options, timeliness, prudence, or communication; they only want an opponent.

They don't want variety; they want a villain on whom they can project all the evil and oppression that they feel weighing upon their souls. That's why they only need two tribes. One is "us," the heroes; the other is "them," the villains. The villain matters more than the hero, though. He's what is important—he's the scapegoat that the modern man requires to in order to cope. That's why even "our guy" usually isn't that appealing. He doesn't need to be. He only needs to be politically groomed in such a way that he can be used to defeat the great demonic enemy.

The problem is that you and I were born too late to buy into the drama. We look on at the animosity and we can't get excited about it—it disturbs us, but it doesn't move us. We can't tell hero from villain. In fact, we don't even see a hero. We just see two villains. Occasionally, though, we will see each side do something slightly heroic or respectable. In short, we see their contradictions and so we recognize them for what they are: human, flawed, and angry. Neither candidate is the demon that we are led to believe. They might be stupid, bigoted, or hypocritical, but they are only men, and they usually have some redeeming qualities.

So, as was the case with the churches, we do not abstain from the voting booths because we don't care. We simply refuse to put our stamp of approval on a party suit who we know can do nothing for us and who is certainly serving his own moneyed interests. We don't trust him. He has nothing to do with our lives. He's after power, and we don't have any power. All we have is a vote, and even though we don't believe our vote counts, we see no reason to give it away. So we remain silent.

Our political stance is the most practical expression of our doubt. It isn't an inner agnosticism, because at least in this area we know exactly what we think and why we do what we do. Because we know and have passed judgment, we do not participate. We stand apart. We'll participate when there is actually something to participate in.

We see the structure in decay, collapsing. We see the people standing inside beckoning us to enter and join the party (their party, of course). But we can't do it. We don't want the roof to fall in on our heads. If we can someday get enough of them out here with us, we'll give the falling structure the final push ourselves, and send it to the ground. That's the only responsible thing to do with a dilapidated building. You don't want anyone getting killed when it falls on its own. So that's what we'd do. We'd push the whole thing over and build again. But for now there are far too many people still inside, screaming and yelling and angry but refusing to leave. So we stand apart and wait, not indifferent, just patient.

Patriotism

> Americans seem irritated by the slightest criticism and appear greedy for praise. The flimsiest compliment pleases them and the most fulsome rarely manages to satisfy them; they plague you constantly to make you praise them and, if you show yourself reluctant, they praise themselves. Doubting their own worth, they could be said to need a constant illustration of it before their eyes. Their vanity is not only greedy, it is also restless and jealous. It grants nothing while making endless demands. It begs one moment and quarrels the next.
>
> Alexis de Tocqueville[17]

THERE ARE CERTAIN PEOPLE in this world whose fates are unavoidably intertwined with my own. *You*, for example, if you happen to be an American, will always, to some degree, share my fate. We are in the same massive boat. If a foreign enemy overruns our whole nation, you and I will both suffer the ordeal together. If you live in my city and famine or disease strikes, then you will endure the hunger or the fever right next to me.

This is the true basis of patriotism. Understood in this way, it is a beautiful thing worthy of being taught to all men. It creates a sense of brotherhood, a feeling of connectedness, and a framework of community, through which people bind themselves together and support one another simply because they were born in the same town, the same state, or the same nation.

It is as if there were a great chain by which I am linked to you and to the world. The closer I am to you on the chain, the more

17. Alexis de Tocqueville, *Democracy in America* (New York: Penguin, 2003), 710.

intimately our fates are bound; but ultimately it does not matter where a person is on this earth: we are still in some way attached. The earth is nothing more than the ultimate boat which contains all the others. Even though those on the far end of the great chain are so far removed from my life that I will never meet them, they are still there and still connected. One way or another, we are engaged in a great project together, and the ripples of our lives cannot help but intersect.

This isn't some vague spiritualism, and it isn't some poetic ideal: it is just common sense.

Patriotism is nothing more than a term we use to describe our organic responsibility to "our" section of the chain. After all, if the links are to remain strong, each should cling tightly to those nearest. The goal, however, is always connectedness. That is why patriotism, if it is to remain sane, must not be rooted in feelings of separation, otherness, fear, and resentment, but in a desire for association and intimacy. If it departs from this basis and turns instead to rhetoric about superiority, fueling pride, hate, and distance, then it is no longer a true patriotism. It is something else. It is called *nationalism*, which is an almost religious devotion to the State as an idea and an end in itself. It also requires, by its nature, that all other nations be despised and viewed as inferior. Within the spirit of nationalism, only one's own nation has any merit and is worthy of any esteem. Nationalism tells its followers that they live in "the greatest nation in all the world!"—and anyone who questions this superiority is a traitor and a heretic. But now nationalism is a dead word, and it is dead because it took on the name of *patriotism*.

Now, patriotism is no longer something based on responsibility to what has been made mine simply through birth and life in a certain place and time; patriotism is no longer the duty to help my neighbor simply because he is my neighbor. No, that wasn't enough. The new patriotism demands not simply that I look out for my neighbor, but that I shout from the rooftops that my neighborhood is greater than all other neighborhoods, and that I believe myself and my neighbor to be the greatest men in the world.

I don't know about you, but I was happier with the old responsibility. I'll give my neighbor a cup of sugar and a couple of eggs when he comes knocking. I'll help him put out a fire in his house if I must. But I'm not going to act like an idiot, running around yelling about how great we are—my neighbor and I. That's nothing but self-flattery and conceit.

I could have stuck by the old patriotism because it was sane. It was rooted in the responsibilities that come with intimacy, all the way back to the family itself. I must care for my family, not because my family is the greatest and most deserving family in the world, but for no other reason than that it is *my family.*

My family loyalty has nothing to do with its superiority in the world. I know my family too well to live under such illusions about its supposed supremacy. I couldn't say it with a straight face! I don't need those illusions.

What I'm saying is that I don't need appeals to my *pride* to get me to care for my family, and that same truth extends to my neighbor and my nation. I do not need to condescend to the rest of the world in order to be devoted to the land where I live and the people I live among. I can love my nation without hating all others. If I must hate all others in order to love mine, then I do not have love for my nation—I have a diseased pride in it, and that is something else.

My patriotism, if I have any, is a patriotism of community, duty, and love. It must never have anything to do with pride, and the moment it does is the moment I will become ashamed of it.

Pride is the opposite of love, and the modern patriotism, which is just nationalism in disguise, is based on pride. It has become the opposite of what it was when it was sane. If we want to return it to sanity, we must return to a patriotism based on connectedness, responsibility, and, yes, even love. We must turn patriotism back into what it was when it was reasonable, which requires turning it into the opposite of what it is now.

I tell you this because patriotism is another one of those "keywords" of the verbal universe that carries with it an extraordinary power. People will use it against you, and in fact they probably already have used it against you. They use it to shame you into an unquestioning obedience. They use it to kindle within you the basest passions and sentiments. They use it to draw you away from your wives and children, to send you off to some other country to shoot some man you've never met. They use patriotism to do this. If we could restore the word to its true, noble meaning, it could not be abused in such a way. It would become once again a tool of community and togetherness, instead of a tool of pride, bigotry, and division.

War

Our generation automatically perceives all war as unjust. It's almost *a priori*. Seeing this, an observer could be tempted to think that we are principled pacifists. That would be one explanation, but it would be wrong.

The truth is that we *could* conceive of a war worth fighting and which we could get behind, but we have been so suffocated all our lives by wars that are distant, senseless, petty, and based on motivations all too obscure to us. It is by this incessant conditioning that we have become instinctively opposed to war as something dark and suspect. Our aversion to war is not a high ideal, it is a habit. It is a practical pacifism developed through experience.

We are like the villagers in that children's story who heard the cry "Wolf!" too many times and eventually grew tired of the drill. When the bell rings and the watchman cries, "Our freedom! Our freedom is under attack! To war!"—we are instantly skeptical. It isn't that we love the wolves and want them to come destroy the flock; it isn't that we don't believe the wolves exist. We just don't see any reason to believe the village crier. We know wolves are out there; we just don't have any faith in the people responsible for ringing the alarm bell. They've been ringing too long.

That's the second half of the problem: we've become numb to the sound of the bell. It has been ringing so long that we can't hear it anymore. War and the threat of war are just part of our ambience. The propaganda that once roused the passions of the whole populace just makes us nod our heads and change the channel. That's what happens when a society employs propaganda constantly. It loses its potency and becomes counterproductive because no one notices it anymore.

Incessant, pulverizing propaganda. That's all we've ever known. They turned on the machine after WWII and forgot to turn it back off. It rings in our ears twenty-four hours a day.

That's part of the reason we don't even protest the wars that come and go, the way some of our parents protested during Vietnam. In order to protest with that sort of passion, you have to be able to perceive a crisis. No one can get up in arms about their normal circumstances. Plus, you've got to have some alternative in your head so that you can tell yourself: "This is how things *should* be." In other words, before you can identify a bad war for what it is, you've got to be able to identify a good one. You've got to have some notion of what a war based on justice looks like. But we've never seen a just war. We weren't around for Hitler and his Holocaust.

All we've known is what we now have. We've become numb to the whole thing. I suppose that is a blessing, if numbness can ever be considered a blessing. We're at least immune to propaganda. Our passions cannot easily be charged and manipulated. We still lack direction, however. Numbness leaves one confused and inert. At least the victims of propaganda had a direction. We know that the noise of the politician on the loudspeaker isn't for us, but when we walk away our ears are ringing so loud that we can't hear ourselves think and we don't know where we want to go.

That is why we are ambivalent about war. We don't know what a just war looks like, and so we can't identify what exactly it is about this incessant violence that strikes us as evil. We have no comparative background with which to draw our distinctions. Nonetheless we sense something insane behind the march, and the war cry.

"They hate our freedom!"—someone tells us. What does that mean? Who are *they*? Which freedom? The freedom to raise a family and live a good life? Well I suppose that would be a freedom worth dying to protect.

But there are other kinds of freedom we enjoy and which we exercise all too often. What if these enemies of ours hate our freedom to swear and blaspheme in the streets? What if they hate our freedom to exploit the weak; to make debt-slaves out of the desperate and the stupid; to plaster sex all over public spaces; to sell that sex to children; to swallow the entire world's resources through excessive consumption; or to reinforce slavery and abuse in poor countries just to have cheaper amenities? If those are the freedoms under attack, then we won't be so quick to join the cause, will we? We will neither kill nor die defending those liberties.

Freedom is meaningless in itself. It is a word, and a vague word at that. It could mean anything at all. Tell me which freedom is under attack, and why it is worth defending. But please stop insulting my intelligence with your war slogans.

Many of us join the cause, though. Just like many of us go to church, and many of us vote, and many of us work seventy years and then die. We live in the madness and we can't always get around it. For one reason or another, many of us end up with a rifle in our hands in a foreign land.

As usual, we don't join the military because we are enthusiastic about this or that war. We don't join because we are convinced about a particular cause. We join because the military advertises itself as an escape from aimlessness. It promises meaning and victory to generations of men who feel aimless and impotent.

Men, as we said before, seek initiation and trial so that they can know who they are and that they are men. They crave this. That's how the military gets men these days. It doesn't promise death for a just cause, it just offers the possibility of meaning in battle. It hijacks the old assumptions about the warrior life as something disciplined, honorable, and offering man a path to transcend himself. That's exactly what our generation needs, after all. But the modern military is the last place to find it.

I knew a warrior once who joined the military. He thought the military was for warriors. By the time he finished boot camp he saw the lie. He saw military training for what it was: not a trial of manhood but a process of conditioning. He saw that it did not so much offer men principle as it did a program to follow.

The modern military is a unique instance of one of the traditional paths to fulfillment and growth into adulthood which has completely lost its essence while retaining its honorable reputation. It is yet another surrogate initiation for men in turmoil.

Modern militaries do not need men—beings with principles and virtues and powerful wills—modern militaries need men completely devoid of willfulness and spirit. They need soldiers with technical training and conditioned psyches. In a sense, military progress in the last few centuries represents a transformation away from the warrior and toward the "soldier." The great victory of this new military methodology was that it somehow retained all the prestige, offering all the old promises and honors of the classical warrior vocation, even though it had become something entirely different. That's how it continues to draw aimless young men into its net. Every man wants to be a warrior.

And so, many of us join the armed service to fight for our country. We don't do it because we believe in the war, but because we want to believe in something and we think that by fighting we'll be able to rise to that certainty. We go to war to conquer our existential rootlessness. That's when the real barbarism of modern war shows itself.

Remember that love and war are two things which cannot be made clean without making them monstrous. To kill is an evil, but men always tried to keep the evil within limits and to superimpose some sort of honor onto the whole affair. But man has now liberated himself from honor and limits.

They sought to make war sterile, clean, and safe—like "safe sex." The story has the same ending. Now war is more barbaric than ever. A man cannot kill another man safely and without risk or responsibility. If he tries he will suffer consequences the severity of which he may not be able to endure. That's why some of our brothers pick up a rifle, go off to war, and then end up shooting themselves. The whole thing has become spiritual gangrene. No one survives, not even the victor.

Men once killed each other face to face. It was traumatic, it was horrific, and it was not clean. But relatively few soldiers died then, and each life taken on the battle field was felt, whether by friend or foe. It was intimate and personal, even if awful. Then we made progress and man began taking steps back from the battlefield, and the corpses began to pile up. Now one soldier can take any number of lives in seconds. He may not even feel this increase in gore at all—and that is precisely the problem. He can now kill without feeling it so much, and that is a terrible injustice, not just to those being killed, but to the man pulling the trigger. It hides from him the severity of his act. A man should never be able to kill without feeling it and seeing the life that he is smothering.

Just as love cannot be reduced to its physical process without producing monstrous inhumanities, so it is with war. And this is exactly what we've done.

Naturally, the old ideas about "honor" and the "warrior vocation," in which the solider became something like a monk with a weapon, have all but evaporated into thin air. There is no place for them when war is waged with buttons and without personal contact of any kind between enemies. How can a solider respect his enemy when he kills him from a mile off?

Soon, it seems, wars will be fought with machines. Or at least that's how it will work for the rich nations. Already the poor technicians who must manipulate the death machines from a computer and then return to their families, as if nothing had happened that day, are suffering the consequences of this inhumanity. Man can remove himself from the field as much as he wants, but killing is still killing, and he'll always walk away changed.

The old strategy was to face the responsibility full force, right in the eyes. Only under such a discipline could a man kill an enemy and salvage his humanity. He faced the trauma of death by doing his best to transcend it. This is why the old warrior vocation had much in common with the priestly vocation, and why knights stood all-night vigils in church before pledging their swords to a cause. Modern man tries to salvage his humanity not by embracing the severity of the act but by escaping it. It leaves him all the hollower the farther away he is able to remove himself. If he stands a vigil, it is in front of a flag rather than before the cross.

Responsibility is inescapable. You may run, but it will overtake you in the end, wherever you go. Modern warfare, from its motivations to its methods, seems to us a grand effort to escape responsibility.

Now they want to take the women to these wars as well. They call it "equal opportunity." Equal opportunity means that our daughters, and not just our sons, will go off to fight the next world war.

And they wonder why we have no taste for the whole thing.

Mass Living

Where men live huddled together without true communion, there seems to be greater sharing, and a more genuine communion. But this is not communion, only immersion in the general meaninglessness of countless slogans and clichés repeated over and over again so that in the end one listens without hearing and responds without thinking. The constant din of empty words and machine noises, the endless booming of loudspeak-

> ers end by making true communication and true communion almost impossible. Each individual in the mass is insulated by thick layers of insensibility. He doesn't care, he doesn't hear, he doesn't think. He does not act, he is pushed. He does not talk, he produces conventional sounds when stimulated by the appropriate noises. He does not think, he secretes clichés.
>
> Thomas Merton[18]

EVER WONDER WHY OUR GENERATION has an infatuation with zombies? Think about the scenario: it is always a world where the hero is nearly or completely alone; he is also nomadic with no place to call home, simply wandering through the ruins of a once-human civilization in which all the other people have become monstrous and hostile. These once-human creatures move slowly through the streets, anonymous, devoid of anything resembling a personality, and harmless, until you get too close, at which point you'll be eaten alive. The hero must exist in this ambient ménage, trying to make the best of what he can scavenge, with little hope of ever finding an idyllic, peaceful, human life. The old ways of fellowship and happiness are shut, even though the earth is still spinning and most of the people are still there.

What does that all sound like? Is that not a caricatured but frighteningly accurate depiction of modern man's existence in the crowd? That's why our generation loves the zombie flicks. We can, in a very sick way, relate. The story speaks to us more than the old John Wayne cowboy-and-Indian conflict. We've moved on.

John Wayne was a drifter and loner, just like our apocalyptic heroes; but his solitude was of an entirely different character. The

18. Thomas Merton, *New Seeds of Contemplation* (New York: New Directions, 2007), 54–55.

noble, rootless cowboy was in solitude because he walked away from civilization. He was menaced by Indians; he deserted those like him and wandered into alien territory. His solitude came from being alone by choice: he could have chosen differently.

Our new loneliness—the loneliness we like to see in our zombie hero—is of a very different kind. It is a loneliness of immersion within a mass. We see people, we move within crowds of them, even bumping into them on the subway, but we don't know them as people. We cannot know them, and so we live largely in solitude. And there is no alternative. It isn't a matter of choice.

This is an expression of the frustrations of mass existence. Just look at the structures we build ourselves.

We live in hives—that's really the only word to describe apartment buildings and skyscrapers. They're hives. We live in closer proximity to our fellow men than ever before, and yet we don't know our neighbors at all. That's our paradox. You live next-door to me but I know nothing about you, and to be honest I don't want to know you. If you lived a mile down the road then perhaps I'd like to meet you, but I need distance between us first. If I'm going to be glad to see you, I have to be able to see you coming before you bump into me on the elevator. When I must unwillingly rub up against you every day, when I must hear you on the other side of my wall every night, then cannot desire to meet you because you are already too close for comfort.

Our presence in the hive means we are automatically invasive toward one another. It drives out or at least inhibits communion even when we really do desire it. Isn't this true, my fellow resident of the hive? How is your little cell over there, by the way?—can you hear me typing? Perhaps one day, when this tower of Babel collapses and we're driven out into the open air, we'll be able to meet for the first time.

That's what this is, by the way, this skyscraper filled with a hundred cells. It is the tower of Babel. We have lots of them. They are great achievements of human genius, wondrous structures to impress the entire world and reach to the heavens!—and they destroy the possibility of real human communication. That's Babel for you, to a T. It doesn't matter if we all speak English. Within the hive we might as well all be from different planets.

What always confused me about the myth of Babel was that each man seemed to have received his very own language—his very own confused tongue. But it all makes sense when I look at us, in our great and wonderful structures. If you put too many men together in a room and get them all going, then it matters very little that they all speak the same language. It doesn't help them one bit! Their communication is still babble, and their tongues are confused.

My point is merely this: you and I, if we ever want to meet, if we ever want to get away from the babbling, we will have to give up the hive life. That won't solve all of our problems, but it will solve at least one.

Maybe the men at Babel became zombies; or, if they didn't, I'd bet each man felt like he was surrounded by zombies. Either way, zombies or babbling fools, I think we can relate. This is what the sociologists mean when they say that modern men are "mass men." We are a mass. We are living as an undifferentiated confusion of humanity.

The Environment

> I can have no confidence in places where the air is first fouled and then cleansed, where the water is first made deadly and then made safe with other poisons.
>
> Thomas Merton[19]

> The way humanity treats the environment influences the way it treats itself, and vice versa.
>
> Pope Benedict XVI

THE DEBATE ABOUT CLIMATE CHANGE has got it all wrong—both sides. It's wrong in every way.

The basic question, as it is put before us, is about whether or not man is capable of destroying the earth and with it his own species. One side argues that man can in fact do this by exhausting the earth's resources and natural balance, and concludes therefore that we need to protect the environment if for no other reason than self-preservation. The other side seems to think that man does not wield that kind of power, at least not yet, and so we can continue to do whatever we will without thought of limits or concern for consequence.

Isn't the whole spirit of this argument disturbing?

We should not need to be convinced that the earth is certainly going to die before we try to keep it beautiful. I shouldn't need to have it statistically proven to me that a species is going extinct before I give consideration to its flourishing. There should be some appreciation for beauty, life, harmony, and balance within

19. Thomas Merton, *Raids on the Unspeakable* (New York: New Directions, 1964), 10–11.

me that drives me to care for the earth in such a way that the question of its extinction never comes up. A civilization that has to be convinced that extinction is immanent before they will act as ministers to their own garden is already lost.

Think about the madness of it all, dear reader. I do not clean my kitchen just because the failure to do so will result in disease and death. I do it because a clean living space is more attractive and brings me a sense of peace and order.

I don't abstain from littering because I think I'm going to kill all the animals on the side of the road with my trash. I don't need to think about that at all. I choose not to litter because it would feel like leaving food to decompose on my furniture. It's childish and sloppy. It probably isn't going to kill anyone, but that isn't the point. I'm not two years old.

But that's what the debate about global warming sounds like to my ears. It is a debate between two-year-olds who absolutely must have proof that the world is ending before they will clean up their rooms. It's embarrassing.

The ecological problem is not a problem of carbon emissions, soil depletion, and habitat destruction. Those are all involved, but they are accidental and secondary. The real problem is that we have become a civilization that places no value on beauty, limits, life, and harmony; we can only value utility, production, and base pleasure.

I cannot say that the science is valid or invalid—I'm agnostic about global warming. I know only this: whether or not the water levels in the ocean are rising or falling, I'd prefer that the beach not be covered with filth. Whether or not the temperature of the water is changing, I'd prefer it be filled with a wonderful variety of life. I like gardens, forests, clean rivers, and pastures.

Whichever side wins this whole global warming debate, it is a loss for us, because it is a loss for beauty. It will prove that only an argument based on utility, or on the threat of death, can get anything done. It will show me that those things I value most are, to my society, not considered worthy causes for action.

Immigration

THIS ISSUE IS VERY MUCH RIDICULOUS to us. For one thing, we know that our forefathers invaded this land and destroyed an entire civilization with no regard whatsoever for its traditions and its way of life. The native people were driven into extinction, if not in fact, at least in practice, living on in the new culture only as a museum piece, only less-respected and not so carefully preserved. Now we hear cries of anger and lamentation about a new race of invaders wandering across our border and threatening our "traditions" and our "way of life." To us it seems like cosmic irony, really, or even, in a way, justice. To see things any other way would require us to discard what little historical self-awareness we have.

That's why we have trouble getting on board. It isn't that we don't treasure our roots and our small semblance of culture. It isn't that we don't understand the problems of illegal immigration. It's just that we see the contradiction at the same time and all too clearly. We know our history, and we can't even begin to condemn poor immigrants without feeling that we ought also to condemn ourselves.

Yes, yes, I know that it has been a couple hundred years since we took this land by conquest, and so there is little sense in talking as if we could undo it or make up for it. I only mention the idea of deportation to express what we feel and not what I think we should actually do. The problems of our day must be addressed as they present themselves to us, and not in light of a past which cannot be altered or undone.

Still, we feel this past acutely, and, let me say again, we are ultra-sensitive to hypocrisy.

For example, they say these immigrants are taking money out of our economy. Yet the wealthiest, most legally "American" businesses among us do precisely the same thing via foreign banks as a means of escaping the social responsibilities attached to their wealth. These immigrants are taking valuable "jobs"? Even if we admit that the work they do qualifies as employment and not slave labor, our largest corporations export jobs that are far more comfortable and far more legitimate every year, and with less justification, since they do not have the pressure of poverty upon their shoulders.

We can't open our mouths to criticize an alien without those sharp pangs hitting us in the gut, reminding us that we aren't being quite authentic. This makes the issue of illegal aliens much more of a conundrum to us than it seems to be for our parents, many of whom seem to have no qualms about condemning these evil foreigners for their lack of appreciation and respect for the existing institutions of our nation.

I only mention this issue briefly because it is *our* issue. It is part of our landscape and it is something we'll have to deal with in our own way. We may not use any of the answers currently bouncing around on the television and between the parties. That's the main reason I wanted to talk about this issue. We'll find our own answers, you and I, once we decide which direction we want to go in this world. That's what this conversation is about, after all: we want to describe, diagnose, and find a direction in which to go. In the meantime, do not let anyone tell you that you cannot empathize with an alien. Regardless of where we go on the issue, your ability to empathize with other people will be your greatest asset, even if many of your elders think it is a liability.

Inebriation and Anesthesia

> I have the feeling that drinking is a form of suicide where you're allowed to return to life and begin all over the next day. It's like killing yourself, and then you're reborn. I guess I've lived about ten or fifteen thousand lives now.
>
> Charles Bukowski[20]

THERE ARE SOME INSTRUCTIVE PARALLELS to be drawn between those things that a man does in order to cope with a reality perceived as intolerable, and those things that a whole society does, collectively, in order to cope with the same thing.

For example, a man who drinks all day apparently has little hope in the prospects offered to him by reality, and so he looks elsewhere for happiness—or, if not happiness, then at least some peace and quiet. That is to say, he drinks simultaneously for pleasure and escape—for inebriation and then anesthesia.

20. During a December 1974 interview with *London Magazine*.

He drinks to insert feelings into his life that he wishes he had while numbing himself to those feelings he has but wishes he didn't. It may fail with respect to the former, but it will never fail with respect to the latter. That is why Bukowski was right in calling it a sort of surrogate for suicide: it offers the same end, a total deadness to reality, without the finality. Deep intoxication is suicide without the commitment. And it's cheap.

The problem is worse if you're young and you haven't developed the thick skin and self-knowledge needed to withstand the soul-sucking chaos around you. To be young, sensitive, and aware, in a world experienced as hollow, inhuman, and absurd, is to be left with no other option than to turn off the mind. You either have to find a way to stop thinking, or else go insane. It is appropriate, in such times, to speak of young men and women who live a "traumatized existence."

There is a third option, of course, which is to close your eyes, play Nintendo, and go with the flow. This is a more passive form of escapism, different only in approach from the violent plunge into oblivion taken by the alcoholic. In this approach, you just keep your eyes on the ground in front of you, day by day, and you may make it through okay. Just don't question anything, and don't, under any circumstances, seek meaningful answers. But lift your head once and you'll be in trouble. You'll wake up into a nightmare and you may not be able to get back to sleep.

Those are your options when you are young and awake. You've got to kill the awareness or else you might kill yourself. That makes alcohol a necessity, because it gives you a little of both.

Young people shouldn't look at the world and see a void of

meaningless activity before them as their only possible future. They don't have the strength or stamina to deal with it.

Now, dear reader: take these notions, if they seem true to you, and apply them to society at large. Society itself has felt these same things and reacted in the same fashion, only on a collective level. It has developed its own collective coping mechanisms and collective anesthetics to numb itself to the same things with which the individual struggles. Thus, while the study of individual self-medication is one thing, there are also phenomena which can be more accurately described in terms of a collective anesthesia.

In fact, a society which seeks anesthesia cooperatively will develop a colorful array of opiates, much more subtle and effective than simple intoxication, in order to satisfy its collective need for numbness. And these opiates, because they are products of the group effort, will be far more socially acceptable than the smell of alcohol on your breath.

Many of these anesthetizing techniques remain completely unconscious and invisible. You participate without consent or awareness of the fact.

Did you ever wonder why we are so frantically moving from place to place all day long, one activity to the next, always busy, busy, busy? No matter where we are, we never seem to be where we'd like to be. As soon as we get where we are going, we discover that where we are is not where we wanted to be after all, and so we leave again. The car, in fact, could be our cultural symbol, because the car is a place you enter and sit in, never because you want to be there, but so you can be somewhere else.

With this in mind, consider the fact that, according to psychiatrists, sheer activity can actually provide a narcotizing effect. This means that feverish commotion, in itself, can offer a sort of desensitization. Therefore, if a society begins living at such a consistently frantic pace, we cannot deny the possibility that it does so in pursuit of just this sort of inebriation.

Modern men hate to stand still. Stillness forces you to become aware of your thoughts and feelings. Activity keeps you numb. Like a drowning man in the ocean, if you flail around enough, you can beat back the waters of awareness; but as soon as you stand still they overcome you and smother you with what you did not want to see.

That sort of awareness is what the alcoholic fears, and that is why he drowns himself in drink. When society collectively seeks the same escape, it adopts a frenetic lifestyle.

So there you go, dear reader. There's one thing to watch out for: Don't be a busy-body, at least not if you want to be able to think; and if you find that standing still terrifies you, you might do well to ask why.

Democracy itself has been transformed into an anesthetic. Democracy is the new "opiate of the people." We already spoke about the scapegoat offered by politics, and about how that is quite literally the only comfort offered by the whole circus with its votes and its villains. It is a grand opiate, and it's free to all. For this one you don't even need a car. Unfortunately for us, this great anesthetic is losing its potency. It is a psychological opiate and requires a degree of belief. We don't really believe in it any more, and so it offers us no escape. In fact, election time just reminds us of how impotent we really feel. You might say we are becoming "resistant" to the democracy drug. It doesn't give us the high that it apparently gave earlier generations. So we keep looking, and we find other ways to benumb ourselves.

Television, for example. Television is a paradoxical anesthetic because it stimulates while it stupefies. It gives you a feeling of excitement and lethargy at the same time. It is thus the symbolic anesthetic for a sedentary civilization. It stimulates your mind just enough to steal your sleep, but it stupefies you just enough to make sure you don't actually do anything with yourself during that time. That's why couples with television sets in the bedroom get less sleep but also have less sex.

Television mesmerizes. You can forget yourself when you've got the TV on. In the end, that's precisely what we're after. TV allows you to ignore your loneliness. That's what the laugh tracks do—and that's why we need them. People don't like to laugh when they are alone. Laugh tracks are the only thing keeping lonely people laughing, which is to say, keeping lonely people from acknowledging their loneliness.

So many opiates. Even kids get narcotics these days. All the stimulation flying around and pulverizing their little senses, and then they are sent to school and expected to stay still and pay attention to what is quite possibly the most boring, hollowing educational experience yet devised. Not surprisingly, they can't endure it. So we give them a diagnosis and a drug made for children. Lots of us were anesthetized from our earliest years.

Alcohol isn't sounding nearly so bad after all that, come to think of it. It seems that the guy drinking alcohol isn't so strange after all. He just knows better what he's after, and he wants it more. He wants to escape, just like everyone else. And to forget. Everyone wants to forget themselves.

Homo Economicus

> Ancient politicians talked incessantly about morality and virtue; our politicians talk only about business and money.... They assess men like herds of livestock. According to them, a man has no value to the State apart from what he consumes in it.
>
> Jean-Jacques Rousseau[21]

ALL OF THE THINGS we've talked about so far hang together—or perhaps it would be better to say that all these things *work together*: all of these social trends, all of these spiritual pressures, all of these existential tensions converge into one overwhelming force, resulting in the creation of a very specific *type of man*, to the exclusion of *all other human types*.

I'll call this distinct type of man the "economic man," or *homo economicus*. I believe this term is appropriate because the type we are discussing is a man devoid of any concerns, dimensions, passions, and pursuits beyond the acquisitive and material—which is to say the *economic*—ones. Nothing else matters, either for him or his society.

Other pursuits, such as the religious or moral, may be proclaimed in the streets, in the pulpit, or on the political campaign

21. Rousseau, *Discourse on the Arts and Sciences.*

by this type of man—but we are not concerned with his hollow rhetoric. We are concerned with what this man and his civilization actually pursue and actually practice; and in this respect it is appropriate to speak of a purely "economic man" as the general type fostered by our present civilization.

That is the world into which we have been born: a society far advanced in all forms of material wealth, but working actively toward the exclusion of all *extra-economic values*.

For this society—our present society—anything which cannot be reduced to purely economic terms is denied the right to exist. Everything is judged in terms of efficiency, affordability, functionality, production value, "standard of living," etc. This strictly economic framework dictates the nature and direction, not only of society as a whole, but even of our own individual aspirations.

I'm not talking about the superficial desire for material possession, dear reader. Greed is included here, but it is just one symptom of the disease which lies at the heart of *homo economicus*.

The true essence of the problem is *an economic experience of life and everything within it*, from "relationships" to sex and even to religion. We are taught to judge and experience our own goals, truths, beauties, and pursuits in light of and through this dead, cold, mathematical, transactional framework, which is to say, by using the measures that are purely economic.

Think about the problems we've explored. Remember the abstract and imaginary entity called the "person" which has come to replace the concrete and colorful realities of "men" and "women"? There is only one place in which this sterile, gender-neutral thing can actually exist, and that is in economics. Economics can deal with persons—in fact, it must deal with persons, because it cannot deal with men, women, and children.

This is what I mean when I say that our own mentality, down to our deepest perceptions of ourselves and others, has been impoverished into conformity with an all-encompassing *economic worldview.*

Man has reduced his understanding of himself to his role as economic participant: he is producer, consumer, employee, employer, or party of a contract. No needs are valid beyond those directly related to his physiochemical machinery.

Again, we are not just talking about money and business!

Remember what we said about "relationships"? The word itself is an economic term. It is something that can only be accounted for and judged within the economic framework.

In future histories they will say that *homo economicus* came after *homo sapiens*. If they are wise, they'll also say that, although he came after, he was below *homo sapiens*. They'll say he was a degraded form of humanity which forced man to summon all his power in order to overcome it.

It is incredibly ironic that some people are outraged when evolutionists link them to primates. Those men feel that being placed next to an animal on some evolutionary chain has removed their dignity as human beings. And yet how many of these same indignant men and women wake up every day and embrace this baser role as *homo economicus*, the "physiochemical actor" whose pursuits are perhaps even more predictable and one-dimensional than those of the apes.

Homo eocnomicus is perfectly predictable, in spite of, or perhaps because of, all his productivity. He is predictable like a productive ant building an anthill, working hard but for no higher purpose than to make the hill bigger.

Remember "mass man" and his grand hives a hundred stories tall?—men piled on top of one another in their towers? They touch one another without meeting, and hear one another without speaking. That's *homo economicus*—living with spectacular efficiency—just like the ants.

The more we explore this phenomenon, which is *the slow elimination from society of every pursuit that is not economic*, the more we see how deeply it has penetrated the spirit of our era.

What place does beauty have in our civilization? It certainly isn't reason enough to care for the environment. For that we need threat of death and extinction. But even with that set aside, beauty still has no role and no power of determination in our pursuits.

Look at the architecture of the past. Everything is beautiful. It is as if men couldn't so much as build a stairway without embellishing it in some fashion, leaving the accent of their human personality on the finished work. Everything reflected a concern for the beautiful. Everything we build is ugly. It's all squares and boxes. It's efficient.

Art has no role in the life of *homo economicus*. It can only be found in special "galleries" where you go to see beauty divorced from use, which is an inferior type of beauty. Galleries might be best understood as paradoxical museums of the now, where we put things which, although they were created today, are already anachronisms. All art in our age is an anachronism. That's why we must go to galleries to see beauty, isolated and protected as if it were a curiosity for an interested and sometimes eccentric few.

Homo eocnomicus also develops his own language, wholly of external relationships and transactional logic. For example, when we say someone is "successful," what do we mean? We mean that he has made lots of money, and usually nothing more. That is the language of *homo economicus*, and we use it daily.

This mentality shapes our very notions of the mind and of knowledge. *Homo economicus* is not wise—he is "smart" or he is an "expert" at something. You see, he cannot be "wise" because wisdom is not reducible to a quantity of facts that can be accumulated and then judged. Wisdom is therefore meaningless. *Smart* and *expert*, on the other hand, denote quantities of data. That's what we economic actors need: quantities of data. Our education has been shaped accordingly. Gone is the philosopher, the Galileo and the Archimedes, whose knowledge ranged across all subjects. Today the only path to "success" is to be "specialized," so that you can "market" yourself in a certain field for which there is a "demand," depending on "scarcity" in that profession.

And so we follow the path of *homo economicus*, many of us, because we do not know what else to do. We live this out our entire lives, but part of us remains aware that the whole program is without meaning, just an organized chaos with nothing underneath but the dust to which we must eventually return. We feel the complex structure of our industrial society, precisely arranged and calculated; and yet we simultaneously sense something a little insane and ominous about it. We feel that it moves towards some imminent destination, but we aren't sure if that destination is paradise, or just a longer shift at the assembly line, and so we are more than a little anxious about the situation.

But that's all underneath, in our depths. As for what we can see with our eyes, it's all just about making the anthill bigger.

What do we hear every day in the news, in every board meeting at work, and at every State of the Union Address? We hear about how we need "growth." And what do we need to grow? The "economy." That is our perpetual project, because the economy, that abstract thing which has proven more mysterious than any of the old gods, feeds all the "persons."

We are the "persons"—the "individuals." We are *homo economicus*, and we work our whole lives to feed and fatten the great Sacred Cow, the *economy*. Nothing that threatens the primacy of the Sacred Cow has a right *to be*, or at least not *to be* in any meaningful way, and neither are we allowed to pursue such things. No extra-economic value can stand in the presence of this god.

Perhaps it's time we turn the tables. Instead of worshipping the fat cow so that it will give us silver spoons with nothing on them, I say we toss the spoons and eat the cow. We've been feeding it long enough. Tear it down from the pedestal and have at it, and we might even find that, contrary to all of our fears, there is plenty to go around. Then we can turn to new pursuits—more human pursuits. With the false god dead and our stomachs full, we can go forward and decide what type of men we really wish to become.

Mythopoeic Man

> ...we must begin with the Myth, the penultimate truth, of which all experience is the temporal reflection. The mythical narrative is of timeless and placeless validity, true nowever and everywhere... just as in our still told myths, 'once upon a time' does not mean 'once' alone, but 'once for all.' The Myth is not a 'poetic invention' in the sense these words now bear: on the other hand, just because of its universality, it can be told, and with equal authority, from many different points of view.
>
> Ananda Coomaraswamy[22]

> Inevitably the myths woven by us, though they contain error, will also reflect a splintered fragment of the true light, the eternal truth that is with God. Indeed only by myth-making, only by becoming 'sub-creator' and inventing stories, can Man aspire to the state of perfection that he knew before the Fall. Our myths may be misguided, but they steer however shakily towards the true harbour, while materialistic 'progress' leads only to a yawning abyss and the Iron Crown of the power of evil.
>
> J. R. R. Tolkien[23]

22. Ananda K. Coomaraswamy, *Hinduism and Buddhism* (New York: Golden Elixir Press, 2011), 7.

23. Humphrey Carpenter, *J.R.R. Tolkien: A Biography* (New York: Houghton Mifflin, 1977), 151.

Against this deviated form of humanity, *homo economicus*, we have to offer some alternative, something more open-ended and capable of giving expression to man's full range of possibilities. My suggestion, which I will share with you now, is a human type I call "Mythopoeic Man." The term means literally *myth-making* man. Here, however, it will be used to mean much more—it will be used to convey an entirely new experience of life.

One of our many prejudices is to automatically understand the word "myth" to mean "that which is not true." Such a definition is only accurate if we assume that myths, as they've been handed down to us, were intended to explain our reality in precise literal, historical terms. Such a superficial understanding of the matter, I'm afraid, was never the reality in those ancient societies that actually created and used myths. The myth was never meant to convey such simple things as historical facts.

A myth is a special kind of narrative by which men explain themselves to themselves. A myth may take place in a historical, physical setting, but that context is nothing but the "carrier" for the message, used as a device to convey a truth which lies elsewhere, above and beyond time and place. In that sense, mythology is very near to poetry. Like poetry, if a person reads the work only for its grammar and sentence structure, he is going to miss its point entirely.

Perhaps I can explain better by way of example.

Consider for a moment the myth of Actaeon, a skilled huntsman who stumbles upon the beautiful Artemis while she is bathing in a cave. Actaeon immediately flees from the presence of the goddess whose beauty he has unintentionally beheld, but he cannot escape the consequences of what he saw. The goddess curses him and, as he runs away, he is transformed into a stag. He calls out to his friends who were out with him that day. They see him, but can only perceive the stag he has become. They assail him, as do his own dogs, and because he cannot speak with a human tongue to tell them who he is, he is torn to pieces by his own friends and animals, who can no longer recognize him.

Now anyone can see that there is in this tragic tale a chronological series of events which could entertain children and just about anyone else with its characters, twists, intrigue, and excitement; but it is an act of gross superficiality to assume these things are all the story holds. To make that mistake is to miss the point of all mythology.

There is imbedded in Actaeon's tale, beneath the fiction, a profound truth about the human condition which is not accessible to the shallow, but which can be heard by all those who *have ears to hear*. Anyone who has ever undergone an existential crisis or a life-changing moment of epiphany knows that the intimate experience of truth encountered at that moment changed him forever. When you walked away from that experience of truth or beauty or light or whatever it was, the world looked different. Some of your former loves had lost their beauty; some former friends may have become enemies. But it was not the world that had changed, but you yourself, and the world was only responding to your transformation. Things which once brought you joy may now bring you pain.

How many of us have our own pack of dogs hunting us in the night—wild passions that once made us happy but which we now try to escape at all costs? And what brought about this painful change? Often it was a vision of beauty, of love transcendent, of a woman, a poem, an illness, or an encounter with the Almighty that brought on this change and cast a new light on our entire being.

That is the nature and purpose of mythology: that it remains true for every man and woman who ever lived. What does it matter that there was never, in fact, a man named Actaeon who became a stag? That was never the point. He does not need to exist *in fact*, because he exists in our inner reality—and that is *more true than fact*.

We were led to believe that our science has shown us the real truths that the old myths, with their ignorant stories, failed to see—but is it not really the other way around? Myths show us the truths that are beyond fact, and which science could never hope to show us. Myth and science attack the same problems, but they use entirely different approaches. Myth is a human-based, personalistic approach; science is a matter-based, fact-superstitious approach used by *homo economicus* because anything subtle has become invisible to him. The scientific approach is wonderfully effective at dealing with dead things, but wholly inadequate when dealing with man. We were taught that science, with its facts, offers us "the truth behind the myth"; but it is perhaps more accurate to say that it is the myth which offers us "the truth behind the fact."

Now perhaps we can begin to appreciate Mythopoeic Man—this *myth-making*, personalistic, poetical, all-embracing human type—who is capable of piercing his own depths and of choosing social ends which can satisfy his highest aspirations.

It should be obvious that I'm not trying to argue for some simple story-teller. I mean nothing of the sort. This man is mythopoeic due to his sense of life and his mentality toward the world. I'm speaking of a whole man whose approach to life is comprehensive enough to grapple with all of reality, with its mysteries and its contradictions. For this man to exist, he need not create myths literally and in narrative form; he need only be of the type that can understand them if he encounters them, and who could possibly create a myth if he needed to.

What a feat it is to create a myth, and to own a mythology! To own a mythology is to have a framework through which to understand man in mind and spirit, and not just in body. Then perhaps *wonder* would again be able to exist in our horizon.

Only the most profound soul is capable of translating the interior depths of humanity, which are the depths of us all, and then expressing that truth in art, architecture, music, or in a story so simple and accessible as the tale of Actaeon the hunter! This is no man of mere nursery rhymes, trying to teach children the "moral of the story." This man—my Mythopoeic Man—if he is allowed to exist will finally be capable of creating a human culture and communicating to his neighbors and his offspring the things which are most important to men.

This man is the heart of all culture, whenever and wherever he exists, and his absence is why we have no culture to speak of. Mythopoeic man is *the* bearer of culture—of art, song, literature, craft, and philosophy. Mythopoeic man does not just create stories; the storyteller is just one role played within the mythopoeic civilization.

The weaver who takes his weaving as his holy vocation and transforms his "job" into an art is also a member of this whole and healthy type. He does not have to tell any tales—he is piercing depth and sharing his own inner myth through his simple craft. The builder or the architect—they too are myth-makers, although their myths are expressed in stone and wood, playing with space and height. Everything done or created in such a civilization is marked with the accent of mythopoeia, which is to say it has meaning as well as function.

Remember our lament about the ugliness of our architecture, with its dead logic and empty functionality? Mythopoeic Man would not dream of it—he couldn't dream of it. Beauty and function are always fused for him. There is no such thing for him as a good house that is not also an attractive house. Utility and truth are fused for him, because his life is whole.

Saying the same thing another way, he is *creative*, and not just *productive*. That's why they used to say that man was made in the image of God, you know. God is the archetype of the creator, and man was once a miniature replica of that creative fire, wielding his little trident with joy everywhere he went. *Homo economicus* is right when he thinks that all the talk about the "image of god" is strange and silly. It is silly, *for him*, because it does not apply to him. He discarded the teaching, not because it never applied to man, but because it ceased to apply when man reduced himself to a being who only produces, consumes, and then produces again.

I offer you the notion of a whole being. Call him what you want, it doesn't matter. He is whole.

His soul is not something he has to think about. He is not trapped in his head, rationalizing his life away. If he falls down to worship, he does not do so in order to "get in touch with his spirituality." His experience of life *is* his spirituality. It isn't something he has to chase down. He is a human being, body, mind, and soul: he cannot be accounted for in terms of only one of his parts.

Because he is not trapped in his mind, he is unified and personalistic. He is able to handle contradiction in a way that the rationalist never can. He feels himself as merely human, yes, because that is what he is, but also as something more, something inexplicable and grand; and he can take this mystery in stride. His ability to revel in mystery and contradiction is perhaps his greatest advantage. It means that he can cope with everything he sees, since contradiction is everywhere. He does not demand precise logical conformity and reasonable explanations for everything. He is too sane to expect all that.

He is comfortable in a world that doesn't make sense. Thus, peace is possible for him, not because he is ignorant and lacks the use of his mind, but because he is not superficial enough to demand that everything fit nicely between his ears. Humanity is a limited creature, and because this man knows his limits, he embraces mystery. By embracing mystery, he experiences wonder.

Homo economicus cannot handle any contradiction—it is indigestible to him and, his very constitution rejects it. He must either deny whatever seems contradictory, or he must live with the agony of trying to maintain two opposed notions in his head. Those are his only options: denial or suffering. He cannot be whole. *Wonder,* for him, is immediately transmuted into frustration and fear. He is at a disadvantage and has undermined himself from the start.

And so we return to our present generation. We are *homo economicus*: undermined, uncertain, incapable of dealing with our existence. I am not quite arrogant enough to say that we *must* choose *my* model as our new ideal; but we will have to choose something that is similar to it. If we can agree on that much, then we can talk about how exactly one goes about making such deep and far-reaching changes.

Automatism and Free Will

> Freedom is completely without meaning unless it is related to necessity, unless it represents victory over necessity. To say that freedom is graven in the nature of man, is to say that man is free because he obeys his nature, or, to put it another way, because he is conditioned by his nature. This is nonsense. We must not think of the problem in terms of a choice between being determined and being free. We must... say that man is indeed determined, but that it is open to him to overcome necessity, and that this act is freedom. Freedom is not static but dynamic; not a vested interest, but a prize continually to be won. The moment man stops and resigns himself, he becomes subject to determinism. He is most enslaved when he thinks he is comfortably settled in freedom.
>
> Jacques Ellul[24]

THE FIRST STEP IS to build a *culture of consciousness*, aware of what it is doing, where it is going, and why.

24. Jacques Ellul, *The Technological Society* (New York: Random House, 1964), xxxii–xxxiii.

In order to do this, we first have to acknowledge that there is more to consciousness than being awake and walking around. You can be awake and walking without being conscious, sort of like sleepwalking. You can be unconscious and still make a peanut butter sandwich.

I'm not kidding either. Epileptics who experience periodic seizures may have a seizure while in the middle of some very complex routine, which they will continue to carry out to completion even while unconscious. So long as you know where the peanut butter was, and so long as you've buttered bread before, you do not have to be conscious in order to make the sandwich. That's how the brain works.

One epileptic was a pianist who was known to experience attacks in the middle of his practice sessions. He would pause momentarily, which is how his parents would know the seizure had occurred, and then would continue to play the song to completion with great dexterity.

What I'm trying to say here, dear reader, is that consciousness, real consciousness, is a rare thing, much rarer than you might think. Just because you drove your car to work this morning does not mean you were conscious. The brain, through habit and training, can carry out most of life's activities on its own, absent your guidance. When this kind of unconsciousness reaches an extreme, as was the case with the epileptic, the person enters a state called *automatism*.

The automaton, or man-as-automaton, can carry out any action with which he is familiar, although such an individual will usually be incapable of processing new data or reacting to changes in circumstance. The program of the brain is running, but the programmer is no longer at the controls.

Obviously there can be various "degrees of consciousness" between full automatism and true awareness, which leads us to wonder how often men actually live in what could be called a conscious state. The answer is important, for free will is impossible without consciousness.

The automaton can't make any meaningful decisions—the automaton cannot direct itself to a certain purpose or end. The automaton can only respond to stimuli, and even then it only reacts through previously learned routines. The automaton is absolutely conditioned. If this description sounds familiar, it is because it represents precisely the modern scientific vision of man in general. Man in general, according to our psychologists, is always, more or less, the automaton.

This is why science denies the existence of free will. If man is always and everywhere the automaton, then he does not have free will.

What a crime against humanity that was, teaching us as children that we had no free will and no capacity for purposeful action. They had their reasons, our educators. Their denial of free will is understandable, in light of what man has come to believe about his nature in recent centuries.

But in the end they answered the wrong question. The question is not, "Can man act as a free, self-determined agent?"—but rather, "How often does he actually do this?" The reason our predecessors answered the first question in the negative was that they did not think to ask if it were possible to consider free will only as a potentiality and not as an all-or-nothing, universal characteristic.

Man can and does go through his entire day acting automatically, thinking of nothing that he did not think of yesterday, answering no questions he has not already answered before, and directing himself to no purpose other than habit and self-indulgence. Our predecessors, those great scientists, saw him doing this, and drew the *selectively true but not universally true* conclusion that man has no free will at all. Because so many men were indeed living the life of the automaton, I suppose we cannot be too hard on them. They were only doing what scientists do: observing what men do, and drawing conclusions based on those observations.

We don't have to believe them, though, you and I. We can understand them, empathize with their error, and then correct it. If we don't, then it will become a self-fulfilling prophecy. Convince a man that he is an animal, and he will be much more prone to act like one. Once man accepts that he is driven by instinct and routine, he will be incapable of seeing anything more—not in himself or in anyone else. Only the man who goes against himself and beyond himself knows that there is a free will to be had.

Scientists were right when they denied free will in some men, but they were wrong in denying it to all men. They were right when they saw that consciousness is rare, but wrong in saying that it is non-existent. They had spent too much time watching men butter their bread, watch the news, vote, work, sleep, and butter more bread. They had spent too much effort measuring responses to stimuli. They had been too long observing *homo economicus*. When all you see is *homo economicus*, then free will truly is extinct and the scientists are justified in all their conclusions.

It is time to talk of consciousness, and to seek wakefulness. This is why every tradition of wisdom talks endlessly about wakefulness; it is why so many sages and wise men seemed to have undergone an "awakening" at one point or another. The sage knows that a man may very well live much of his life in terms of an existence that is barely more than bovine. Man can, if he allows it, be animated by nothing more than Freudian sex drive, animal instinct, and environmental determinations. Everyone has always known this much; science didn't teach us anything in that regard.

The difference is that the old wisdom assured us that another life was also possible, and spent all its time trying to encourage us to seek this alternative existence. They taught us to seek a life "awake" and thus capable of being filled with meaning, a conscious life in which the free will exists and is in frequent and joyful use.

✦

So what shall it be, dear reader? Automatism?—or something better? You do have a choice. The automaton will always exist and be open to you as an option. It is useful, after all, when you are making a peanut butter and jelly sandwich. You can't discard the automaton completely. It is good, so long as it isn't the end of the story.

The terrible injustice of our education was to teach us that the automaton was the end, even if it only taught us this by neglecting to mention anything else. The result of such an education has been that very often the automaton is the end, becoming that self-fulfilling prophecy of impoverishment. A generation trained to think of themselves as determined by nature is almost guaranteed to act accordingly.

Our job is to spare future generations that terrible impoverishment of possibilities. Our job is to bring back the rest of the story—to find out what lies beyond the automaton, and to teach the free will to the next generation. Our job is to destroy the barrier that has been erected, humiliating man by telling him that he can go no further than environmental determination and instinct. That is the Berlin Wall of our epoch, telling man that he may live only on his animal side, and may never enter the realm of the human. It shouldn't be too hard of a wall to smash.

Answering the Question

> Most modern freedom is at root fear. It is not so much that we are too bold to endure rules; it is rather that we are too timid to endure responsibilities.
>
> G.K. Chesterton[25]

> Freedom is only part of the story and half of the truth. Freedom is but the negative aspect of the whole phenomenon whose positive aspect is responsibleness. In fact, freedom is in danger of degenerating into mere arbitrariness unless it is lived in terms of responsibleness. That is why I recommend that the Statue of Liberty on the East Coast be supplemented by a Statue of Responsibility on the West Coast.
>
> Viktor Frankl[26]

25. G.K. Chesterton, *What's Wrong with the World* (London: Dodo Press, 2010), 105.

26. Viktor E. Frankl, *Man's Search for Meaning* (New York: Simon & Schuster, 1963), 209–210.

OUR FIRST STEP had to be a rediscovery of the will, because the will is the highest faculty and it is the only thing that makes a purposeful life possible. To allow the will to atrophy, or to deny its existence, is to deny all meaning.

If you can get that far, opening yourself once again to the possibility of meaning, then your next step is to orient this new faculty in a particular direction. This is the beginning of freedom, that "freedom" which everyone has been shouting about but rarely understood. So many of those who argue about freedom and liberty do not even have the beginnings of either. Now you have the beginnings, and you have to direct this power to a purpose.

In short, you have to answer that impossible question about your freedom: "Free for what?" Which is just another way of asking: "Alive for what?" If you can answer for your freedom, you can answer for your life, and if you can't answer for the one then you can't answer for the other. They are the same answer, because the essence of humanness is freedom and will. Every thing else hinges on these powers, even love. Without the possibility of choice, we cannot choose to love.

To say the same thing another way, to have the power of the will is to have responsibility. A predetermined being cannot be responsible in the true sense. That's why so many people choose the automaton. Having to answer for the breath you take each morning can be a great burden, and so the whole question is often avoided. It is easier that way, and that is perhaps why our predecessors taught us that it was the *only* way. But we've grown tired of easy: we now desire a full, virile acknowledgment of our being, and we don't care if it is difficult.

It *is* difficult. The very nature of the question hurls us into alien territory. It asks us to do what we've never felt able to accomplish: it asks us to find a certainty—to decide to live as if our certainty were absolute—to *believe* in some principle as true, once and for all, choosing to make ourselves responsible to that truth, and directing our lives toward that principle. Answering this question will initiate you into the realm of certainty. There's no getting around it.

It won't be a comfortable position for you. You'll experience an entirely new kind of anxiety, because freedom is the beginning of anxiety. If you have no will and all of your actions are determined by environment and physical law, then you cannot really have any impact on the universe. That is a great relief, in many ways. Not so with freedom. The idea that your words and deeds, however small, can affect human history is deeply disturbing.

A life of potency brings with it a new kind of pain, but it is pain with purpose, and that is why it is worth enduring. Until now the turmoil and chaos you've suffered has been the pain of absurdity, with no end, no beginning, and no meaning behind the madness. It was suffering without hope. A life of freedom brings the great weight of responsibility; but it is a wonderful burden because, although it is heavy, it actually allows you to move about, whereas before you were powerless and inert. This new burden, then, is not a chain to weigh you down; it is your anchor which allows you to choose when to ride the waves and when to stand firm. Responsibility is the chain that sustains.

So make your answer: "Free for what?"—and chain your freedom to that answer. That answer is your first certainty, whether it be beauty, wisdom, faith, justice, mercy, peace, or love. Let it be the directing principle of your life and it will lead you to all other certainties in time. It is only the beginning, your first glimpse of solid ground after life in the ocean of doubt. Find this solidity and hold onto it. If you do not tether yourself to a purpose and a principle, remaining of your own will responsible to it, then you will be flung back into the abyss; or else you will become exhausted in your search and fall back into the sleep of automatism, not wanting to wake again even if you could.

A New Peasantry

> I bid you to a one-man revolution
> The only revolution that is coming.
>
> Robert Frost[27]

I FEAR THAT I MAY HAVE seemed a bit grandiose in my aspirations, what with all the talk of mythopoeia and a radical new man for a radical new civilization. But I want you to know that my aspirations are not at all fantastic. They are actually quite humble. In fact, that is what is so radical about them: simplicity is radical in a world colored by mad hubris.

Mythopoeic Man is no Nietzschean superman, and neither is he a Plato or a Galileo. He isn't even a saint. I need you to know that he is one of the simplest of men, and to convey this to you I want to describe him in another light and by another name: I want to offer you the idea of Mythopoeic Man as *peasant*. This means also that my exhortation to a new, more human, civilization could be framed as nothing more than a call to a New Peasantry.

27. Robert Frost, *Build Soil: a political pastoral* (1932).

I use the word "peasant" only partly because of its historical reality. I do believe the historical peasant was a noble creature, but I choose the word primarily because of the *feelings* and *sentiments* attached to it in contemporary language. It is packed with negative connotation and it emphasizes all the material and spiritual prejudices we carry with us. It rings in our ears and leaves a nasty taste in our mouths. It is a term which speaks very loudly, then, and in this context does much of my talking for me. For us, the peasant is something low, ignorant, sad, poor, and pitiable. Those are the meanings the word carries for us. That's why we cringe at its usage. We cringe because it challenges us by presenting a lifestyle that defies all of our presuppositions about what man needs to be happy, at peace, and comfortable. Everything that our economic civilization emphasizes, the peasant disregards and proves unnecessary. Everything that our political ideologies raise as essential, the peasant moves along without. Everything that consumerism teaches us to crave, the peasant scorns or laughs at. He gives the lie to our civilization.

That is why he is such a useful model for us. He is useful not because he is perfect, but because he is a perfect *corrective* to the modern aristocratic ideal of superficial luxury. He no doubt had his faults, but his faults were the opposite of those reinforced by our civilization today. The peasant ideal is a remedy for our extremes, and an excellent device for tempering our attitudes. Such an ideal can offer us alternative perspectives which can then expand our horizons, allowing us to judge and question our values in a new way.

We could say, for example, that a peasant is not one who lives in poverty—he is one who lives simply. A peasant does not live in ignorance—he is one who perceives the world around him as it is, and as he encounters it every day. A peasant does not feel needy as you or I do—he knows what the word "need" means, and so he knows how few needs he actually has. He finds that those needs are few, and his peace lies in knowing how easily those few can be met. A peasant is not unambitious—he is one who, knowing his own heart, does not stretch himself beyond his limits and try to live a delusion. A peasant is not apathetic—he is content.

I long to be a peasant. That is my aspiration, although I consider it very lofty and know that I am far from achieving the goal.

Of course, not everyone need be a peasant. I only offer it as a possible type to complement and clarify all the reflections in this letter. There may be other types—that's the whole beauty of the Mythopoeic framework. It allows for variety. Once we discard the funnel of the modern world and the modern school, it can be replaced with a celestial web of variety and color. We might again see the artisan, another type non-existent in our period. We might begin to see streets lined with shops that are also workshops, men with trades, who create what they sell, and are not confined to only the creating or the selling. We might see, here and there, a true craftsman, and perhaps he will even come to replace the "Craftsman" tool that took on his name after replacing him.

We might see guilds form again before our eyes, associations in which there are no such thing as "jobs," but only masters and apprentices. We might drive into extinction the abomination of work known as the "factory," to be replaced by an economy not of production but of vocation.

My human civilization allows for variety, which is to say, it allows for humanity. But it requires, as a foundation, that the modern mentality of greed, insecurity, artificial need, and endless ambition be replaced by something very different. The new civilization will have to be founded on the peasant ideal.

Truly, dear reader, there is no ideal loftier than the peasant ideal, with its ambitious humility, peaceful discipline, and its ceaseless readiness for celebration and festival. The mythopoeic nature of the peasant soul prepares him for all sorts of contradictions, and he takes them all in stride. He is able to truly live. He takes the day off for a Holy Day, but spends it drinking with his neighbors. He is not a monk—he is a man, but he is usually a religious man. No class of people ever partied like the peasantry. Boredom, that affliction the modern man fights every day to escape, does not enter into the picture.

And self-consciousness? The peasant is one of the few men able to properly digest the apple. Only the peasant mentality can have certainties, because the peasant is also comfortable with mysteries. Such a man always knows what he does and why he does it because he also allows that there is much he does not and cannot know. He can answer for everything, especially his freedom, while hardly having to think about the question. He is the type of man who knows himself, and can therefore live in peace.

Breaking the Vicious Circle

We've spoken about ourselves long enough. Now we may finally move on to the realm of the *practical.*

It was necessary, though—all that talk about ourselves and our condition. If we did not first make sure we understood ourselves, we would have no business trying to better ourselves, and much less would we have any business trying to change the world for others. You can't dig your way out of an avalanche until you know which way is up. If we had started in the practical we'd have probably dug ourselves deeper into the snow. But we are ready now, I hope.

You may regret it, though. Answers to abstract questions are easy: when I tell you what's wrong with your head, you can handle that easily enough. Practical answers aren't of that kind, however. They can't just be taken in through the ears. They're demanding. Practical answers, if they are true, are a summons.

So brace yourself, dear reader, for your summons.

I'll give you the most difficult answer first. There will be others—easier answers, and less demanding—that follow. But I want to give you the most important answer first, because nothing else will have any effect unless you are able to accomplish this one impossible task. It is the simplest, too: *you have to close the schools.*

I told you that you wouldn't like the sound of it, did I not? But there are not a few wise men who have suggested precisely the same thing. One such eloquent voice was the American novelist

D.H. Lawrence. Because his literary powers are greater than my own, I will allow him to expound on this particular point:

> "...we really can make a move on our children's behalf. We really can refrain from thrusting our children any more into those hot-beds of the self-conscious disease, schools. We really can prevent their eating much more of the tissues of leprosy, newspapers and books. For a time, there should be no compulsory teaching to read and write at all. The great mass of humanity should never learn to read and write—never.... And instead of this gnawing, gnawing disease of mental consciousness and awful, unhealthy craving for stimulus and for action, we must substitute genuine action.
>
> "The top and bottom of it is, that it is a crime to teach a child anything at all, school-wise. It is just evil to collect children together and teach them through the head. It causes absolute starvation . . . and sterile substitute of brain knowledge is all the gain. The children of the middle classes are so vitally impoverished, that the miracle is they continue to exist at all. . . .
>
> "I don't want my child to know that five fives are twenty-five, any more than I want my child to wear my hat or my boots. I don't want my child to know. If he wants five fives let him count them on his fingers. As for his little mind, give it a rest, and let his dynamic self be alert. He will ask 'why' often enough. But he more often asks why the sun shines, or why men have mustaches, or why grass is green, than anything sensible. Most of a child's questions are, and should be, unanswerable. They are not questions at all. They are exclamations of wonder, they are remarks half-sceptically addressed. When a child says, 'Why is grass green?' he half implies. 'Is it really green, or is it just taking me in?' And we solemnly begin to prate about chlorophyll. Oh, imbeciles, idiots, inexcusable owls!
>
> "By the age of twenty-one our young people are helpless, hopeless, selfless, floundering mental entities, with nothing in front of them, because they have been starved from the roots, systematically, for twenty-one years, and fed through the head.

> They have had all their mental excitements, sex and everything, all through the head, and when it comes to the actual thing, why, there's nothing in it. Blasé."[28]

Let me now try to justify this notion, which sounds to the contemporary ear like nothing short of madness.

The *status quo* is our greatest enemy. In a democracy, the status quo rules supreme, and the conventional wisdom is an almost invincible force. Our only choice is to find a way to render the status quo impotent and toothless, unable to inject its venom into the young minds of fresh generations.

The logical consequence, then, is that our task must be an educational one. In order to break the vicious circle of indoctrination through which the young are converted into the sleepwalking, will-less *homo economicus*, we've got to break the single institution by which the status quo is handed down. This means that we have to dismantle the school entirely.

You will struggle with this notion perhaps more than with anything else I've said so far. That is how deep the conventional wisdom runs in our democratic blood. Such an idea as this sounds completely absurd; but it is the only way, I assure you.

The school is in fact the living symbol of the status quo. Within the school the child is taught that everything we've rejected in this letter is unquestionably true. Within the school the child is

28. D.H. Lawrence, *Fantasia of the Unconscious* (Rockville: Serenity, 2008), 70–71.

taught to think and speak only within the *verbal universe*, which he will then depend upon for the rest of his life.

There he is taught that he is a *person* and an *individual*; that sex is a physiological process; that he is to be patriotic, work all his life for a successful "career," kill foreigners when the government calls, vote, and, most importantly, spend his money according to what he sees on television.

Upon entering school the child is capable of wonder. He is a genius of creativity, and has goals for his life which, although childish and ignorant, represent his vigor and spiritual integrity. He has human aspirations, even if they are unrealistic in the concrete form he gives them. When the child says he wants to be a fireman, he is saying he wants to do meaningful work which challenges his manhood, allows him to grow in courage, and impacts others in a meaningful way. In this sense, he knows exactly what he wants, and what he wants is a human existence. School destroys all that, eliminating all the highest of his aspirations and ensuring that, by the time he emerges, nothing will remain but the hopes and dreams of *homo economicus*. He will desire money, and will learn to judge his success or failure entirely by that measure.

Do you not see, dear reader, that no revolution in yourself or in your home will have a lasting impact while this institution operates? The school is the modern parent, after all. Children spend the majority of their waking hours being formed in its walls. Once the child enters it, its power will override any doctrines learned at home. It is an impossible adversary if it is allowed to survive.

Children go into the schools as little myth-makers, beings of utmost potentiality, all human possibility operative and open before them; and they come out *homo economicus*, speaking the language of the verbal universe. They'll be able to communicate with their elders and talk about the market, about politics, about reality TV, about income mobility, about financing their first home, about what sort of car they're going to buy, etc.

They'll have become productive, informed, successful, and spiritually neutralized. Their fiery minds will have grown dark, and all the darker if they proceed on to some college.

That is what the school inflicts upon the child's soul. It isn't intentional. It isn't the fault of the teachers, who are usually good people, sensing the error and injustice of what they are forced to do.

That is another tragedy of the "school system"—that even if the teachers see what is happening, they cannot stop it, because it is the only type of education we allow in our civilization. Everything must conform to our economic-industrial existence. That is why our schools will always be this production-model, uniform, homogenizing, lot manufacture "system."

You must close the schools. No, you cannot try to pass some legislation and "fix" the schools. You and I both know such options as government intervention are not possibilities, because the government itself has a vested interest in the status quo. School is the place where you learn to trust the government, after all.

No!—you cannot wait, trusting that things will change naturally sooner or later. You should be through with faith in automatism.

If you find out that smoking causes cancer, then the only wise decision is to stop smoking. If you can only say, "I won't stop until you tell me what I can smoke instead!"—then you are an idiot. Again, if you are driving toward a cliff and someone warns you about the danger, they shouldn't have to offer you an alternative route in order to get you to stop. You don't need an alternative at that point. All you need to know is that the cliff is ahead.

School is our mental cancer—and unlike cigarettes, it does not just "increase the chances" that you'll get the tumor: it ensures it. And the disease is always terminal. That's its purpose. It sets children on a course toward spiritual self-destruction. You can worry about an alternative later—first you just need to stop what you are doing. In fact, it is entirely likely that the current establishment is blinding you to any alternative even if there is one. It is very possible that you will never be able to conceive of anything else so long as the present monstrosity looms large, blocking all light from your vision. That is why there is no time to waste and no reason to hold off.

Again, I know how mad this sounds, but do you really want another generation of "mass men?" Then we must at all costs stop cramming all young people into the classroom to be acclimated to the great herd of other child bodies. That's where the process of compaction and impoverishment begins.

Until you have the courage to take drastic steps, then nothing will change. You can't just take baby steps. Baby steps are for babies and politicians.

Did you really think it would be easy? Did you think it would be a walk in the park to right all these wrongs and bring about a restructuring of civilization? If you did, then again you have the status quo to thank for your delusion. The status quo teaches that all you have to do to make the world better is cast a vote. All the evils you sense, all the systems which oppress you, are addressed in the dim sanctity of that little booth with your piece of paper. That is the paralyzing promise you have to get beyond, or you won't get beyond anything.

It is very difficult for a man to reject the system of which he himself is a product. We all have serious difficulty separating ourselves from the institutions and methods that formed us. This difficulty is compounded by the fact that we were taught to think of our "schooling" as one of our greatest privileges, envied by the world. Our privileged education is one with that silver spoon we spoke so much about in the beginning; it is another one of those things we were expected to be eternally grateful for having received.

We were also taught that this education was not only a gift, but a necessity, and that no person can expect to succeed without it. And so we have believed it, even if we never really found it to be true, and we are poised to pass this belief on to the future. That is the vicious circle which must be broken so that the madness can finally end.

If we managed to close the schools, I would call our generation one of the greatest there ever was. To break one's own vicious circle, especially one with as much momentum as this, requires a spiritual virility few generations in the history of man have been able to muster. If we succeed, we'll have created a historical discontinuity as deep as the one which created us.

Remember our shame?—our shame at the fact that we could not help but reveal the lie behind these schools, this economy, this political ideology? That is our shame, and our only responsible option is to use that shame to discover where and how all these "privileges" have actually been curses. Through this we can redeem ourselves by sparing the next generation such suffering. We can produce a generation without shame, or at least without our particular kind of shame.

We have to refuse to ever wave a silver spoon in front of a child's face and tell him how good he had it, now that we know that having silver spoons is not really all that wonderful after all.

Bring the children home. Mankind got along quite well enough without schooling for thousands of years before us. It is an outright lie to pretend that no one can survive without an "official" education. If the child aspires to read and write, then so be it. Such things are only made difficult when we operate on the maddening assumption that they must be facilitated at a certain speed and under rigid classroom conditions. If we break away from the rigidity, we realize that it matters very little if the child moves slowly.

Without schools we might actually discover how useful libraries can be. If a child wants to learn, he can do it quite easily with a book or with a friend. He can't do that now, though. No one recognizes autonomous learning as worthy of any consideration at all. Only what has the official seal of the school system receives any consideration, and this seal has little relation to actual intelligence, creativity, and general mental worth.

Spare them the curse of being taught to live in their heads. Let them live, as long as possible, in the real world. Let them meet a horse before they learn its "scientific name" and what its insides look like.

They won't get a job, this next generation? We don't want them to have "jobs," dear reader. We want them to have something much more human than that. If you create the space, then perhaps truly human forms of work can be allowed to spring up and exist, designed for man and not for the Sacred Cow of the economy.

End the superstition of schooling. Bring the children home from the mental and spiritual cesspool, from the indoctrination, from the germs that necessitate continuous vaccinations. How grand an era would it be to have children at home again, where they do not need prescription drugs just to cope with the monotony. Mythopoeic civilization cannot exist without mythopoeic men, and such men will never exist so long as schools are the norm.

New Directions

I PROMISED YOU LIGHTER FARE in the way of *practical action*, and I'll give that to you now.

First, however, it is important that you know that this letter is more about the creation of a new mentality than it is about the development of an "action plan" or political program of any sort. Actions come about of their own accord if the right mentality is there; and if the mentality is absent, then, even if I offered up a list of "practical steps" a hundred pages long, it would be of no use. That's why my first aim in this conversation has been to bring about in you an existential re-orientation, centered on true principles, which would then lead you naturally to strive for a more authentically human existence.

I stuck close to principles because principles are the source of all legitimate purposeful action. To skip to the action would have been to start at the wrong end of the whole affair.

Second, I am reluctant to provide "practical advice" because any change in your personal behavior needs to be the dynamic product of your own judgment, because only you know where your particular aptitudes and talents could best be utilized. What is appropriate for me in our cooperative project of change might not be appropriate for you—and what is appropriate for you may not be necessary or healthy for me. Each must do what he can, but there are many trees in the forest; each must bear its own particular kind of fruit. What if, by my own limitations, I offer you an agenda of apples and it just so happens that you are most suited to the production of oranges?

If I say that an excellent first step is to read an old book—Plato, for example—well, then, I might be very right in that suggestion; but I will probably only be right in regard to a certain number of people who possess the particular temperament and aptitudes which would make the study of Plato a beneficial endeavor.

No specific suggestion is universally suitable, and so you must understand that as I enumerate the following possibilities, it is with the full knowledge that they may not apply to you as an individual. They are precisely as I said—they are *possibilities* for new directions:

† Clausewitz said that war was but the "continuation of politics by other means." Our task is one of that kind, in that it demands we proceed *by some other means*—but the means we require lie beyond both politics *and war.* Our strategy must be entirely unconventional. This means, for the time being, that our political posture must be one of *apoliteia*, which means simply "detachment" or "indifference." You must remove yourself from all the hollow rhetoric of the party-mob, so that you can do what those parties and politicians have for so long left undone. Have nothing to do with parties.

† Abstain even from the voting booth, not because voting is necessarily harmful, but simply because it is a waste of time, and because it provides you with a false sense of self-satisfaction which is in no way justified by the act. By denying yourself that indulgence you will be driven to find other contexts in which to act on your social ambitions, and such actions will certainly be more fruitful than the vote you have sacrificed.

† Opt out of the verbal universe of propaganda. The men on the street will still try to bludgeon you with clichés and nonsense, just like they bludgeon each other. But at least you can opt out. When someone talks about "freedom," ask him which freedoms, and for whom. Perhaps then you might actually have a real conversation. Usually, though, you will find it necessary to remain silent, and to practice *apoliteia*, not because you do not wish to participate, but because you know that there is nothing going on in which to participate.

† If you do this—if you opt out—for a substantial period of time, you'll be amazed at the way everything strikes you when you finally return. You'll watch a presidential debate, and for the first time you might realize that they aren't really saying anything at all—they're just throwing out slogans and clichés, appealing to different groups of people with familiar keywords and talking points. Watching the news may actually cause you pain due to its belligerent mindlessness. You'll know that you've changed in some way, and all it took was a period of abstinence.

† Assert also your independence from those technologies which tend to enslave. You don't have to swear off anything for good. Again, as was the case with voting, it is sometimes important to practice abstinence if for no other reason than achieving clarity of vision and renewed perspective. It reminds you that true liberty is freedom from dependence, and you are likely dependent on many superfluous electronic gadgets.

† Deactivate your cellular phone for a year or so. Mobile phones are convenient, certainly, but it is extremely unlikely that you actually "need" one. At first you'll feel the nakedness of not having that lump in your pocket, and then you'll feel the refreshing liberty that comes from not having to ask yourself where that little device is at every moment of every day. You'll be able to walk out the door without your cell-phone-leash tugging at your neck.

† Deactivate your cable television. Throw away your television remote. Re-arrange the furniture so that your living room actually becomes a "family room" where people can face each other, rather than a "television room" in which your family congregates merely to sit in silence as the pictures flash.

† Get the television out of your bedroom, especially if you are married. The consequences of this action will not be unpleasant.

† Go listen to live music—music that is human and emitted directly from human beings, rather than the digitized and falsified electronic sounds produced by speakers.

† Bring musicians back into existence to replace the cult of celebrity that now produces your music. Musicians and any true artists cannot exist in our current regime except as novelties and "celebrities," because our world does not demand the real presence of musicians for its music.

† Make your own music. Learn an instrument, or sing.

† Grow something—and then, if it is edible, eat it. There is something spiritually nourishing in seeing something through from its beginning to its end. It shows you the artificiality of the fast-food chain. It shows you that real food grown by hand is not perfectly shaped and colored, free of all blemish—and you will

understand that it tastes all the better for its blemishes. You will understand the whole story of what you eat.

† Trade your lawn for a garden. If you do not have an official "garden" space because your nice lawn is in the way, then destroy your nice lawn. Rip it up. Neatly trimmed lawns, all mowed in uniform diagonal strips, are the preoccupation of bored aristocrats. The peasant would never tolerate a sprinkler system and a fertilization routine just to have a greener lawn than the guy next door. Tear it up down to the roots, and turn the whole thing into a garden. There are plenty of individuals doing just this already. Follow their lead, and bring color and beauty that changes with the season, rather than the meticulous, monotonous turf field you have growing right now.

† Build a library. There is no better escape from the hidden prejudices of your time than to immerse yourself in another period of history, exposing yourself to men who questioned many of the things you take for granted, and who took for granted many of the things you question. Even if you are an expert on your own age, you are still largely ignorant if you remain within that age only.

† Read a book on logic. Through this you'll immunize yourself against much nonsense.

† Study the concept of propaganda. Jacques Ellul would be an excellent start. Learn how the media machinery works to condition your mind. Learn how

advertisements manipulate your appetites. See what people take you for.

† Write a letter to a friend. Emails are not letters—neither are phone calls. Letters are a fusion of art, effort, and affection, and they convey intangibles that cannot be sent to an "inbox."

† Have a child, even if you aren't "financially stable." Have two, actually.

† Throw away the contraceptives and the condoms. You aren't a stray animal that needs sterilization. If you must avoid pregnancy, then just abstain during fertility, and make love the rest of the month. You'll transform each month into a period of courtship followed by a honeymoon.

† Give birth at home. Reclaim the business of being born from the medical technicians. When it comes time to bring a new life into the world, do it at home, away from the cold, dispassionate sterility of the hospital.

† School your child at home, slowly, at a natural pace. Remarkably little is really needed in order to survive in this world, and for those few necessities, school usually just gets in the way. The majority of mankind got along well enough without literacy anyway, and in such a way was spared much literary trash.

† When it comes time to die, die at home as well, surrounded by your own things and your own family. You

> do not need a doctor to help you die. That is the one moment when doctors become utterly useless, and their presence absurd.
>
> † More importantly, stop what you are doing and reconcile yourself with death. Ready yourself for it, and make sure that when it comes you are capable of accepting it as a natural phenomenon. Know that you've lived, and why you've lived, so that when the end comes you are larger than the moment and are able to leave this world with dignity, rather than clinging to the last vestiges of existence as if you thought you'd live forever. Decide now what it means to live a "whole" life, and live that. A whole life does not have to be long in order to be full; and if a life is not whole, no amount of time would ever feel long enough.

There you are. That's a start, at least. Remember, these are only possibilities. Many more possibilities may occur to you, and I have no doubt they'll be more suitable to your condition than the ones that have occurred to me. Go then and carry out what you discern. Just don't be stupid or narrow about it: don't assume that your aptitudes and aspirations should be shared by everyone. Most of what you do you may have to do alone. It doesn't mean you are wrong, nor does it mean everyone else is wrong, so long as we are working to the same end and for the same principles.

And don't hold everyone else to your standard. It is a great sign of wisdom not to demand from everyone the same things we demand from ourselves. Do what you can with yourself, and look always for others you can combine with in cooperation, sharing yourselves and your talents.

Epilogue

I'VE LEFT MANY THINGS UNSAID in this letter, but most of them were unsaid on purpose. For example, I did not talk very much about God.

The reason for that was simple: *God is dead.* Nietzsche's immortal insight was correct, from a cultural-descriptive point of view. The philosopher was only making an obvious observation about the modern man and his modern disaster—that he lives in a world where God is not acknowledged in any way beyond the occasional internal obeisance.

That's why I didn't write to you to talk about religion and Jesus Christ. I couldn't write to you about that. You've seen the name of Jesus blasphemed, ignored, and patronized every day in your post-Christian civilization. I have no wish to assault you any more with that sort of thing. In our culture, God is a superstition.

And yet I *am* religious—I am a religious man, but I also know that, because of our circumstances, I am on an indefinite pilgrimage. I travel to the Temple, but I do not know when I'll get there. I'll get there, of course, but I don't know when, and I won't pretend I'm there when I'm not.

That's all that a religious man can do in a world where God is dead: he must live as one on a savage, barbarous pilgrimage, even though he may go to church on Sunday mornings.

That's why this conversation was not meant to be evangelical, at least not in the way that word is taken today. *God forbid* I ever write an evangelical book. My generation does not need evangelical literature, and much less does it need what they call "apologetics," designed to trap men more than ever in their own heads with rationalism and argumentation.

The whole point of this conversation was not to *save* you, dear reader, but to *meet* you—to speak to fellow travelers on this savage pilgrimage.

This letter is pre-evangelical and perhaps even pre-Christian, for the simple reason that I am speaking to a post-evangelical and post-Christian people. And so I say again that, whatever this letter could have been, it could never have been *evangelical*.

I want to meet you, first and foremost, before I tell you that you "need Jesus in your life." I will not risk hiding the Gospel from you by trying to insert its facts into your head.

Maybe you don't need Jesus in your life—at least not in the superficial way that many armchair evangelicals mean it.

Or perhaps you *do* need Him—that man in whom I believe—but you don't need to hear about Him from me because you've heard it all before.

Perhaps you are wiser than I, and you see too many of my own ridiculous contradictions, and so you can't take me seriously as a thinker, much less as a spiritual guide. Perhaps I just need to shut up and let you pursue truth without me trying to tell you how to do it, eh?

I acknowledge full well that there are many people walking

around me whose journey I could only hurt by opening my mouth. I could open my mouth, but the only truth they would draw from that experience would be that I do not know or understand them at all.

If I don't preach the Gospel, it is because I am not a missionary or a priest. No one who is not a missionary or priest should preach the Gospel.

As I told you, I am a peasant with a pen and some contemplative leanings. I'll share with you my contemplations, but I won't try to save your soul on my own steam.

If you drop this book and walk away, I'm not going to damn you.

On the contrary: I'll make excuses for you to the end. I will make brilliant excuses, because we are kindred spirits, you and I. As members of the same generation and the same nation, you are "mine" in a very real, patriotic, sense. My patriotic allegiance is not to my nation, but to *you*. That's why I'll defend you.

I'll blame your impoverished civilization; I'll blame your stultifying, soul-destroying education; I'll blame your mind-numbing work; I'll blame the demons.

I'll blame a thousand things, but I'll defend you to the end.
Why? Because I understand what it means to live in a sustained spiritual crisis—sustained for so long you've forgotten all about it. So many of us have forgotten about the struggle and the yearning that gives life its savor and makes it worth living.

The soul, like the body, can only experience trauma for so long before it goes into shock and becomes numb. It chooses not to feel rather than be left feeling nothing but turmoil and frustration. When I look at the modern man, I see a traumatized generation, so accustomed to his rootless existence that his suffering has ceased to register as pain.

That is why I'll argue with God on your behalf. I can't speak for God, of course. But I can speak *to* Him. And that's what I'll do, making excuses for you all the while.

Perhaps God will smile on us then, and we'll see that such a moment was precisely what he had been waiting for all along—waiting for that day when men would stand by each other and plead each other's case in His presence, not so that He'd show Mercy, but so that we could, for at least that one moment, see in each other the Mercy that He had been showing all along.

Maybe then we could know Him again, because we'd know Him in each other.

Daniel Schwindt

Made in the USA
Lexington, KY
28 September 2015